Catholic Teaching
on the Environment

Celebrating the Fifth Anniversary of Laudato Si'

United States Conference of Catholic Bishops
Washington, DC

Cover image: CNS/Paul Haring.

First Printing, May 2020

ISBN 978-1-60137-653-4

Contents

SACRED TRADITION: PRAYERS OF THE CHURCH

The Magisterium

VATICAN II

✺ Pastoral Constitution *Gaudium et Spes* ✺ (*On the Church in the Modern World*)

Principles for Ecological Discernment

Spiritual Roots of the Ills That Afflict Us

Although he was made by God in a state of holiness, from the very onset of his history man abused his liberty, at the urging of the Evil One. Man set himself against God and sought to attain his goal apart from God. Although they knew God, they did not glorify Him as God, but their senseless minds were darkened and they served the creature rather than the Creator (cf. Rom 1:21-25). What divine revelation makes known to us agrees with experience. Examining his heart, man finds that he has inclinations toward evil too, and is engulfed by manifold ills which cannot come from his good Creator. Often refusing to acknowledge God as his beginning, man has disrupted also his proper relationship to his own ultimate goal as well as his whole relationship toward himself and others and all created things. (no. 13)

Discerning the Heart

[One] plunges into the depths of reality whenever he enters into his own heart; God, Who probes the heart (cf. 1 Kgs 16:7; Jer 17:10), awaits him there; there he discerns his proper destiny beneath the eyes of God. (no. 14)

The Role of Conscience and the Law Written on One's Heart

In the depths of his conscience, man detects a law which he does not impose upon himself, but which holds him to obedience. Always summoning him to love good and avoid evil, the voice of conscience when necessary speaks to his heart: do this, shun that. For man has in his heart a law written by God; to obey it is the very dignity of man; according to it he will be judged.[9] Conscience is the most secret core and sanctuary of a man. There he is alone with God, Whose voice echoes in his depths.[10] In a wonderful manner conscience reveals that law which is fulfilled by love of God and neighbor.[11] In fidelity to conscience, Christians are joined with the rest of men in the search for truth, and for the genuine solution to the numerous problems which arise in the life of individuals from social relationships. Hence the more right conscience holds sway, the more persons and groups turn aside from blind choice and strive to be guided by the objective norms of morality. Conscience frequently errs from invincible ignorance without losing its dignity. The same cannot be said for a man who cares but little for truth and goodness, or for a conscience which by degrees grows practically sightless as a result of habitual sin. (no. 16)

9   Cf. Rom 2:15-16.
10   Cf. Pius XII, Radio Address, March 23, 1952.
11   Cf. Mt 22:37-40; Gal. 5:14.

"Govern the World with Justice and Holiness"

Throughout the course of the centuries, men have labored to better the circumstances of their lives through a monumental amount of individual and collective effort. To believers . . . this human activity accords with God's will. For man, created to God's image, received a mandate to subject to himself the earth and all it contains, and to govern the world with justice and holiness; a mandate to relate himself and the totality of things to Him Who was to be acknowledged as the Lord and Creator of all. Thus, by the subjection of all things to man, the name of God would be wonderful in all the earth. (no. 34)

Greater Grace and Power Means Greater Responsibility to Build Up

[Men and women] can justly consider that by their labor they are unfolding the Creator's work . . . and are contributing by their personal industry to the realization in history of the divine plan.

Thus, far from thinking that works produced by man's own talent and energy are in opposition to God's power, and that the rational creature exists as a kind of rival to the Creator, Christians are convinced that the triumphs of the human race are a sign of God's grace and the flowering of His own mysterious design. For the greater man's power becomes, the farther his individual and community responsibility extends. Hence it is clear that men are not deterred by the Christian message from building up the world, or impelled to neglect the welfare of their fellows, but that they are rather more stringently bound to do these very things. (no. 34)

Respecting the Proper, Scientific Laws of Created Things Honors God

By the very circumstance of their having been created, all things are endowed with their own stability, truth, goodness, proper laws and order. Man must respect these as he isolates them by the appropriate methods of the individual sciences or arts. Therefore if methodical investigation within every branch of learning is carried out in a genuinely scientific manner and in accord with moral norms, it never truly conflicts with faith, for earthly matters and the concerns of faith derive from the same God. Indeed whoever labors to penetrate the secrets of reality with a humble and steady mind, even though he is unaware of the fact, is nevertheless being led by the hand of God, who holds all things in existence, and gives them their identity. Consequently, we cannot but deplore certain habits of mind, which are sometimes found too among Christians, which do not sufficiently attend to the rightful independence of science and which, from the arguments and controversies they spark, lead many minds to conclude that faith and science are mutually opposed. (no. 36)

Hearing the Voice of the Creator

If the expression, the independence of temporal affairs, is taken to mean that created things do not depend on God, and that man can use them without any reference to their Creator, anyone who acknowledges God will see how false such a meaning is. For without the Creator the creature would disappear. For their part, however, all believers of whatever religion always hear His revealing voice in the discourse of creatures. (no. 36)

THE PATH FORWARD

An Ancient Struggle Overcome by Jesus' Death and Resurrection

While human progress is a great advantage to man, it brings with it a strong temptation. For when the order of values is jumbled and bad is mixed with the good, individuals and groups pay heed solely to their own interests, and not to those of others. Thus it happens that the world ceases to be a place of true brotherhood. In our own day, the magnified power of humanity threatens to destroy the race itself.

For a monumental struggle against the powers of darkness pervades the whole history of man. The battle was joined from the very origins of the world and will continue until the last day, as the Lord has attested (cf. Mt 24:13; 13:24-30 and 36-43). Caught in this conflict, man is obliged to wrestle constantly if he is to cling to what is good, nor can he achieve his own integrity without great efforts and the help of God's grace. . . .

Hence if anyone wants to know how this unhappy situation can be overcome, Christians will tell him that all human activity, constantly imperiled by man's pride and deranged self-love, must be purified and perfected by the power of Christ's cross and resurrection. For redeemed by Christ and made a new creature in the Holy Spirit, man is able to love the things themselves created by God, and ought to do so. He can receive them from God and respect and reverence them as flowing constantly from the hand of God. Grateful to his Benefactor for these creatures, using and enjoying them in detachment and liberty of spirit, man is led forward into a true possession of them, as having nothing, yet possessing all things (cf. 2 Cor 6:10.). "All are yours, and you are Christ's, and Christ is God's" (1 Cor 3:22-23). (no. 37)

"Bringing Divine Creation to Perfection"

By his labor . . . [a person] can exercise genuine charity and be a partner in the work of bringing divine creation to perfection. Indeed, we hold that through labor offered to God man is associated with the redemptive work of Jesus Christ, Who conferred an eminent dignity on labor when at Nazareth He worked with His own hands. (no. 67)

The Fathers and Doctors of the Church: Share Earthly Goods

God intended the earth with everything contained in it for the use of all human beings and peoples. Thus, under the leadership of justice and in the company of charity, created goods should be in abundance for all in like manner.[8] Whatever the forms of property may be . . . attention must always be paid to this universal destination of earthly goods. In using them, therefore, man should regard the external things that he legitimately possesses not only as his own but also as common in the sense that they should be able to benefit not only him but also others.[9] On the other hand, the right of having a share of earthly goods sufficient for oneself and one's family belongs to everyone. The Fathers and Doctors of the Church held this opinion, teaching that men are obliged to come to the relief of the poor and to do so not merely out of their superfluous goods.[10] If one is in extreme necessity, he has the right to procure for himself what he needs out of the riches of others.[11] Since there are so many people prostrate with hunger in the world, this sacred council urges all, both individuals and governments, to remember the aphorism of the Fathers, "Feed the man dying of hunger, because if you have not fed him, you have killed him,"[12] and really to share and employ their earthly goods, according to the ability of each, especially by supporting individuals or peoples with the aid by which they may be able to help and develop themselves. (no. 69)

8   Cf. Pius XII, Encyclical *Sertum Laetitiae*: AAS 31 (1939), p. 642, John XXIII, Consistorial Allocution: AAS 52 (1960), pp. 5-11; John XXIII, Encyclical Letter *Mater et Magistra*: AAS 53 (1961), p. 411.

9   Cf. St. Thomas, *Summa Theologica*: II-II, q. 32, a. 5 ad 2; Ibid. q. 66, a. 2: cf. explanation in Leo XIII, Encyclical Letter *Rerum Novarum*: AAS 23 (1890-91) p. 651; cf. also Pius XII Allocution of June 1, 1941: AAS 33 (1941), p. 199; Pius XII, Birthday Radio Address 1954: AAS 47 (1955), p. 27.

10   Cf. St. Basil, Hom. in *illud Lucae* "Destruam horrea mea," n. 2 (PG 31, 263); *Lactantius, Divinarum institutionum*, lib. V. on justice (PL 6, 565 B); St. Augustine, In Ioann. Ev. tr. 50, n. 6 (PL 35, 1760); St. Augustine, Enarratio in Ps. CXLVII, 12 (PL 37, 192); St. Gregory the Great, *Homiliae in Ev.*, hom. 20 (PL 76, 1165); St. Gregory the Great, *Regulae Pastoralis liber*, pars III c. 21 (PL 77 87); St. Bonaventure, In III Sent. d. 33, dub. 1 (ed Quacracchi, III, 728); St. Bonaventure, In IV Sent. d. 15, p. II, a. a q. 1 (ed. cit. IV, 371 b); q. de superfluo (ms. Assisi Bibl. Comun. 186, ff. 112a-113a); St. Albert the Great, In III Sent., d. 33, a.3, sol. 1 (ed. Borgnet XXVIII, 611); Id. In IV Sent. d. 15, a. 1 (ed. cit. XXIX, 494-497).

12   Cf. Gratiam, *Decretum*, C. 21, dist. LXXXVI (ed. Friedberg I, 302).

Giving Good Example as Christians

Christians who take an active part in present-day socio-economic development and fight for justice and charity should be convinced that they can make a great contribution to the prosperity of mankind and to the peace of the world. In these activities let them, either as individuals or as members of groups, give a shining example. Having acquired the absolutely necessary skill and experience, they should observe the right order in their earthly activities in faithfulness to Christ and His Gospel. Thus their whole life, both individual and social, will be permeated with the spirit of the beatitudes, notably with a spirit of poverty.

Whoever in obedience to Christ seeks first the Kingdom of God, takes therefrom a stronger and purer love for helping all his brethren and for perfecting the work of justice under the inspiration of charity.[16] (no. 72)

16   For the right use of goods according to the doctrine of the New Testament, cf. Lk 3:11, 10:30 ff; 11:41; 1 Pt 5:3, Mk 8:36; 12:39-41; Jas 5:1-6; 1 Tim 6:8; Eph 1:28; 1 Cor 8:13; 1 Jn 3:17 ff.

Vanquish Sin by Love

Insofar as men are sinful, the threat of war hangs over them, and hang over them it will until the return of Christ. But insofar as men vanquish sin by a union of love, they will vanquish violence as well. (no. 77)

Peace Arises from Love of Neighbor

This peace on earth cannot be obtained unless personal well-being is safeguarded and men freely and trustingly share with one another the riches of their inner spirits and their talents. A firm determination to respect other men and peoples and their dignity, as well as the studied practice of brotherhood are absolutely necessary for the establishment of peace. Hence peace is likewise the fruit of love, which goes beyond what justice can provide.

That earthly peace which arises from love of neighbor symbolizes and results from the peace of Christ which radiates from God the Father. For by the cross the incarnate Son, the prince of peace reconciled all men with God. By thus restoring all men to the unity of one people and one body, He slew hatred in His own flesh; and, after being lifted on high by His resurrection, He poured forth the spirit of love into the hearts of men.

For this reason, all Christians are urgently summoned to do in love what the truth requires, and to join with all true peacemakers in pleading for peace and bringing it about. (no. 78)

International Assistance to Poorer Countries

Christians should cooperate willingly and wholeheartedly in establishing an international order that includes a genuine respect for all freedoms and amicable brotherhood between all. This is all the more pressing since the greater part of the world is still suffering from so much poverty that it is as if Christ Himself were crying out in these poor to beg the charity of the disciples. Do not let men, then, be scandalized because some countries with a majority of citizens who are counted as Christians have an abundance of wealth, whereas others are deprived of the necessities of life and are tormented with hunger, disease, and every kind of misery. The spirit of poverty and charity are the glory and witness of the Church of Christ.

Those Christians are to be praised and supported, therefore, who volunteer their services to help other men and nations. Indeed, it is the duty of the whole People of God . . . to alleviate as far as they are able the sufferings of the modern age. They should do this too, as was the ancient custom in the Church, out of the substance of their goods, and not only out of what is superfluous. (no. 88)

ST. JOHN XXIII

✤ Encyclical *Mater et Magistra* ✤
(*Mother and Teacher*)

The Church's Social Concerns for Humanity

Elevating Earthly Existence

Christianity is the meeting-point of earth and heaven. It lays claim to the whole man, body and soul, intellect and will, inducing him to raise his mind above the changing conditions of this earthly existence and reach upwards for the eternal life of heaven, where one day he will find his unfailing happiness and peace. (no. 2)

Church's Concern for Souls and Daily Life and Welfare

Though the Church's first care must be for souls, how she can sanctify them and make them share in the gifts of heaven, she concerns herself too with the exigencies of man's daily life, with his livelihood and education, and his general, temporal welfare and prosperity. (no. 3)

Material Goods Are to Be Shared in Justice and Charity

Concerning the use of material goods, [Pope Pius XII] declared that the right of every man to use these for his own sustenance is prior to every other economic right . . . in the objective order established by God, the right to property cannot stand in the way of the axiomatic principle that "the goods which were created by God for all men should flow to all alike, according to the principles of justice and charity" (*Sertum Laetitiae* [*On the 150th Anniversary of the Establishment of the Hierarchy in the United States*]). (no. 43)

St. Gregory the Great: Use Talents with Mercy and Generosity

As Leo XIII so wisely taught in *Rerum Novarum*: "whoever has received from the divine bounty a large share of temporal blessings, whether they be external and corporeal, or gifts of the mind, has received them for the purpose of using them for the perfecting of his own nature, and, at the same time, that he may employ them, as the steward of God's Providence, for the benefit of others. 'He that hath a talent,' says St. Gregory the Great, 'let him see that he hide it not; he that hath abundance, let him quicken himself to mercy and generosity; he that hath art and skill, let him do his best to share the use and the utility thereof with his neighbor'" (*Acta Leonis* XIII, XI, 1891, p. 11). (no. 118)

Agricultural Work and the Majesty of Creation

We are convinced that the farming community must take an active part in its own economic advancement, social progress and cultural betterment. Those who live on the land can hardly fail to appreciate the nobility of the work they are called upon to do. They are living in close harmony with Nature—the majestic temple of Creation. Their work has to do with the life of plants and animals, a life that is inexhaustible in its expression, inflexible in its laws, rich in allusions to God the Creator and Provider. They produce food for the support of human life, and the raw materials of industry in ever richer supply.

Theirs is a work which carries with it a dignity all its own. It brings into its service many branches of engineering, chemistry and biology, and is itself a cause of the continued practical development of these sciences in view of the repercussions of scientific and technical progress on the business of farming. It is a work which demands a capacity for orientation and adaptation, patient waiting, a sense of responsibility, and a spirit of perseverance and enterprise. (nos. 144-45)

Nature's Resources: A Blessing of God's Goodness

The resources which God in His goodness and wisdom has implanted in Nature are well-nigh inexhaustible, and He has at the same time given man the intelligence to discover ways and means of exploiting these resources for his own advantage and his own livelihood. Hence, the real solution of the problem is not to be found in expedients which offend against the divinely established moral order and which attack human life at its very source, but in a renewed scientific and technical effort on man's part to deepen and extend his dominion over Nature. The progress of science and technology that has already been achieved opens up almost limitless horizons. (no. 189)

CAUTIONS

Right Ordering of One's Conscience with God

Let [humanity] make all the technical and economic progress they can, there will be no peace nor justice in the world until they return to a sense of their dignity as creatures and sons of God, who is the first and final cause of all created being. . . . For the right ordering of human society presupposes the right ordering of man's conscience with God, who is Himself the source of all justice, truth and love. (no. 215)

Subdue Nature, But Don't Idolize Achievement or Degrade People

Modern man has greatly deepened and extended his knowledge of nature's laws, and has harnessed the forces of nature, making them subservient to his ends. The magnitude of his achievements deserves ungrudging admiration; nor is he yet at the end of his resources.

Nevertheless, in his striving to master and transform the world around him he is in danger of forgetting and of destroying himself. . . . Pope Pius XI, lamented in *Quadragesimo Anno*: "And so bodily labor, which even after original sin was decreed by Providence for the good of man's body and soul, is in many instances changed into an instrument of perversion; for from the factory dead matter goes out improved, whereas men there are corrupted and degraded" (no. 135).

Similarly, . . . Pius XII, rightly asserted that our age is marked by a clear contrast between the immense scientific and technical progress and the fearful human decline shown by "its monstrous masterpiece . . . transforming man into a giant of the physical world at the expense of his spirit, which is reduced to that of a pygmy in the supernatural and eternal world" (Broadcast Message, Christmas Eve, 1953).

And so the words of the Psalmist about the worshippers of false gods are strikingly verified today. Men are losing their own identity in their works, which they admire to the point of idolatry: "The idols of the Gentiles are silver and gold, the works of the hands of men" (Ps 113:4). (nos. 242-44)

Right Relationship Between Creature and Creator

To safeguard man's dignity as a creature of God endowed with a soul in the image and likeness of God, the Church has always demanded a diligent observance of the third Commandment: "Remember that thou keep holy the sabbath day" (Ex 20:8). God certainly has the right and power to command man to devote one day a week to his duty of worshipping the eternal Majesty. Free from mundane cares, he should lift up his mind to the things of heaven, and look into the depths of his conscience, to see how he stands with God in respect of those necessary and inviolable relationships which must exist between the creature and his Creator. (no. 249)

✝ Encyclical *Pacem in Terris* (*Peace on Earth*) ✝

THE GOODNESS OF GOD'S CREATION

A Marvelous Natural Order

That a marvelous order predominates in the world of living beings and in the forces of nature, is the plain lesson which the progress of modern research and the discoveries of technology teach us. And it is part of the greatness of man that he can appreciate that order, and devise the means for harnessing those forces for his own benefit. (no. 2)

Scientific Knowledge Reveals the Greatness of God

What emerges first and foremost from the progress of scientific knowledge and the inventions of technology is the infinite greatness of God Himself, who created both man and the universe. Yes; out of nothing He made all things, and filled them with the fullness of His own wisdom and goodness. Hence, these are the words the holy psalmist used in praise of God: "O Lord, our Lord: how admirable is thy name in the whole earth!" (Ps 8:1). And elsewhere he says: "How great are thy works, O Lord! Thou hast made all things in wisdom" (Ps 103:24).

Moreover, God created man "in His own image and likeness," (cf. Gn 1:26) endowed him with intelligence and freedom, and made him lord of creation. All this the psalmist proclaims when he says: "Thou hast made him a little less than the angels: thou hast crowned him with glory and honor, and hast set him over the works of thy hands. Thou hast subjected all things under his feet" (Ps 8:5-6). (no. 3)

Created Things Reflect the Wisdom of God

The world's Creator has stamped man's inmost being with an order revealed to man by his conscience; and his conscience insists on his preserving it. Men "show the work of the law written in their hearts. Their conscience bears witness to them."(Rom 2:15). And how could it be otherwise? All created being reflects the infinite wisdom of God. It reflects it all the more clearly, the higher it stands in the scale of perfection (Cf. Ps 18:8-11.). (no. 4)

PRINCIPLES FOR PEACE ON EARTH

Honor the Laws Inscribed in Human Nature

The laws which govern men are quite different. The Father of the universe has inscribed them in man's nature, and that is where we must look for them; there and nowhere else. (no. 6)

Truth Is "More Human" When Enacted by Justice, Perfected by Love

The order which prevails in human society is wholly incorporeal in nature. Its foundation is truth, and it must be brought into effect by justice. It needs to be animated and perfected by men's love for one another, and, while preserving freedom intact, it must make for an equilibrium in society which is increasingly more human in character. (no. 37)

The Common Good Concerns Body and Soul

The common good is something which affects the needs of the whole man, body and soul. That, then, is the sort of good which rulers of States must take suitable measure to ensure. They must . . .

aim at achieving the spiritual as well as the material prosperity of their subjects. (no. 57)

Honor the Moral Order Revealed by Nature

One of the principal imperatives of the common good is the recognition of the moral order and the unfailing observance of its precepts. "A firmly established order . . . must be founded on the unshakable and unmoving rock of the moral law, that law which is revealed in the order of nature by the Creator Himself, and engraved indelibly on men's hearts . . . Its principles are beacon lights to guide the policies of men and nations. They are also warning lights—providential signs—which men must heed if their laborious efforts to establish a new order are not to encounter perilous storms and shipwreck" (Cf. Pope Pius XII, Broadcast Message, Christmas 1941). (no. 85)

Remember That People, and Nations, Are Equal in Dignity

The fact is that no one can be by nature superior to his fellows, since all men are equally noble in natural dignity. And consequently there are no differences at all between political communities from the point of view of natural dignity. Each State is like a body, the members of which are human beings. And, as we know from experience, nations can be highly sensitive in matters in any way touching their dignity and honor; and with good reason. (no. 89)

Peace in Human Hearts

The world will never be the dwelling place of peace, till peace has found a home in the heart of each and every man, till every man preserves in himself the order ordained by God to be preserved. (no. 165)

ST. PAUL VI

⋙ Writings and Teachings ⋘

SIN AND RESTORATION

Exploiting Nature May Harm Humanity

Man is suddenly becoming aware that by an ill-considered exploitation of nature he risks destroying it and becoming in his turn the victim of this degradation. Not only is the material environment becoming a permanent menace—pollution and refuse, new illness and absolute destructive capacity—but the human framework is no longer under man's control, thus creating an environment for tomorrow which may well be intolerable. This is a wide-ranging social problem which concerns the entire human family.

The Christian must turn to these new perceptions in order to take on responsibility, together with the rest of men, for a destiny which from now on is shared by all. (Apostolic Letter *Octogesima Adveniens* [*On the Eightieth Anniversary of Rerum Novarum*], no. 21)

Sin Disrupts the Universal Order

Every sin in fact causes a perturbation in the universal order established by God in His ineffable wisdom and infinite charity, and the destruction of immense values with respect to the sinner himself and to the human community. Christians throughout history have always regarded sin not only as a transgression of divine law but also—though not always in a direct and evident way—as contempt for or disregard of the friendship between God and man, just as they have regarded it as a real and unfathomable offense against God and indeed an ungrateful rejection of the love of God shown us through Jesus Christ, who called his disciples friends and not servants. (Apostolic Constitution *Indulgentiarum Doctrina* [*On Indulgences*], no. 2)

Reestablishing Friendship with God

It is therefore necessary for the full remission and—as it is called— reparation of sins not only that friendship with God be reestablished by a sincere conversion of the mind and amends made for the offense against his wisdom and goodness, but also that all the personal as well as social values and those of the universal order itself, which have been diminished or destroyed by sin, be fully reintegrated. (*Indulgentiarum Doctrina*, no. 3)

⟫⟫ Apostolic Exhortation *Evangelii Nuntiandi* ⟪⟪ (*On the Church in the Modern World*)

HUMANE SYSTEMS AND STRUCTURES

Restoration of the Created Order

Between evangelization and human advancement—development and liberation—there are in fact profound links. These include links of an anthropological order, because the man who is to be evangelized is not an abstract being but is subject to social and economic questions. They also include links in the theological order, since one cannot dissociate the plan of creation from the plan of Redemption. . . . It is impossible to accept "that in evangelization one could or should ignore the importance of the problems so much discussed today, concerning justice, liberation, development and peace in the world. This would be to forget the lesson which comes to us from the Gospel concerning love of our neighbor who is suffering and in need."[61]

. . . A proper understanding of the importance and profound meaning of liberation . . . was proclaimed and achieved by Jesus of Nazareth and . . . it is preached by the Church. (no. 31)

61   Paul VI, Address (Sept. 27, 1974).

Building Up Humane Structures

The Church considers it to be undoubtedly important to build up structures which are more human, more just, more respectful of the rights of the person and less oppressive and less enslaving, but she is conscious that the best structures and the most idealized systems soon become inhuman if the inhuman inclinations of the human heart are not made wholesome, if those who live in these struc- tures or who rule them do not undergo a conversion of heart and of outlook. (*Evangelii Nuntiandi* no. 36)

Christian Renewal—To the Ends of the Earth

The Church constantly renews her deepest inspiration, that which comes to her directly from the Lord: To the whole world! To all creation! Right to the ends of the earth! (no. 50)

⋗ Encyclical *Populorum Progressio* ❦ (*On the Development of Peoples*)

THE ABUNDANCE OF THE EARTH IS TO BE SHARED

"Peoples Blessed with Abundance"

Today it is most important for people to understand and appreciate that the social question ties all men together, in every part of the world. . . . The hungry nations of the world cry out to the peoples blessed with abundance. And the Church, cut to the quick by this cry, asks each and every man to hear his brother's plea and answer it lovingly. (no. 3)

Earth Created to Provide for the Necessities of All

In the very first pages of Scripture we read these words: "Fill the earth and subdue it" (Gn 1:28). This teaches us that the whole of creation is for man, that he has been charged to give it meaning by his intelligent activity, to complete and perfect it by his own efforts and to his own advantage.

Now if the earth truly was created to provide man with the necessities of life and the tools for his own progress, it follows that every man has the right to glean what he needs from the earth. The recent Council reiterated this truth: "God intended the earth and everything in it for the use of all human beings and peoples. Thus, under the leadership of justice and in the company of charity, created goods should flow fairly to all."[20]

All other rights, whatever they may be, including the rights of property and free trade, are to be subordinated to this principle. They should in no way hinder it; in fact, they should actively facilitate its implementation. (no. 22)

20   Pastoral Constitution *Gaudium et Spes* (*On the Church in the Modern World*), , no. 69.

"The Earth Belongs to Everyone"

"He who has the goods of this world and sees his brother in need and closes his heart to him, how does the love of God abide in him?" (1 Jn 3:17). Everyone knows that the Fathers of the Church laid down the duty of the rich toward the poor in no uncertain terms. As St. Ambrose put it: "You are not making a gift of what is yours to the poor man, but you are giving him back what is his.

You have been appropriating things that are meant to be for the common use of everyone. The earth belongs to everyone, not to the rich."[22] These words indicate that the right to private property is not absolute and unconditional. (no. 23)

22   De Nabute, c. 12, n. 53: cf. J. R. Palanque, *Saint Ambroise et l'empire romain*, Paris: de Boccard (1933), 336 ff.

Men and Women in the Image of the Creator, "Engraving" the Earth

[Work] is something willed and approved by God. Fashioned in the image of his Creator, "man must cooperate with Him in completing the work of creation and engraving on the earth the spiritual imprint which he himself has received."[25] God gave man intelligence, sensitivity and the power of thought—tools with which to finish and perfect the work He began. Every worker is, to some extent, a creator—be he artist, craftsman, executive, laborer or farmer.

Bent over a material that resists his efforts, the worker leaves his imprint on it, at the same time developing his own powers of persistence, inventiveness and concentration. Further, when work is done in common—when hope, hardship, ambition and joy are shared—it brings together and firmly unites the wills, minds and hearts of men. In its accomplishment, men find themselves to be brothers.[29] (no. 27)

25   Pastoral Constitution *Gaudium et Spes* (*On the Church in the Modern World*), no. 65.
29   Cf., for example, M. D. Chenu, O.P., *Pour une théologie du travail*, Paris: Editions du Seuil (1955) [Eng. tr. *The Theology of Work*, Dublin: Gill, 1963].

Sharing Resources with the Poor as Love of Neighbor

The superfluous goods of wealthier nations ought to be placed at the disposal of poorer nations. The rule, by virtue of which in times past those nearest us were to be helped in time of need, applies today to all the needy throughout the world. And the prospering peoples will be the first to benefit from this. Continuing avarice on their part will arouse the judgment of God and the wrath of the poor, with consequences no one can foresee. (no. 49)

PRINCIPLES OF ECONOMIC AND SOCIAL DEVELOPMENT

Efforts Toward Productivity Should Better the Human Condition

Organized programs designed to increase productivity . . . should reduce inequities, eliminate discrimination, free men from the bonds of servitude, and thus give them the capacity, in the sphere of temporal realities, to improve their lot, to further their moral growth and to develop their spiritual endowments. When we speak of development, we should mean social progress as well as economic growth. (no. 34)

Technology Should Serve Humanity

It is not enough to develop technology so that the earth may become a more suitable living place for human beings. The mistakes of those who led the way should help those now on the road to development to avoid certain dangers. The reign of technology—technocracy, as it is called—can cause as much harm to the world of tomorrow as liberalism did to the world of yesteryear. Economics and technology are meaningless if they do not benefit man, for it is he they are to serve. Man is truly human only if he is the master of his own actions and the judge of their worth, only if he is the architect of his own progress. (no. 34)

Agriculture

Highly industrialized nations export their own manufactured products, for the most part. Less developed nations, on the other hand, have nothing to sell but raw materials and agricultural crops. As a result of technical progress, the price of manufactured products is rising rapidly and they find a ready market. But the basic crops and raw materials produced by the less developed countries are subject to sudden and wide-ranging shifts in market price; they do not share in the growing market value of industrial products.

This poses serious difficulties to the developing nations. They depend on exports to a large extent for a balanced economy and for further steps toward development. Thus the needy nations grow more destitute, while the rich nations become even richer. (no. 57)

Trade and Economic Development

It is evident that the principle of free trade, by itself, is no longer adequate for regulating international agreements. It certainly can work when both parties are about equal economically; in such cases it stimulates progress and rewards effort. That is why industrially developed nations see an element of justice in this principle.

But the case is quite different when the nations involved are far from equal. Market prices that are freely agreed upon can turn out to be most unfair. It must be avowed openly that, in this case, the fundamental tenet of liberalism (as it is called), as the norm for market dealings, is open to serious question. (no. 58)

Social Justice and Fair-Trade Contracts

The teaching set forth by . . . Leo XIII in *Rerum Novarum* is still valid today: when two parties are in very unequal positions, their mutual consent alone does not guarantee a fair contract; the rule of free consent remains subservient to the demands of the natural law. In *Rerum Novarum* this principle was set down with regard to a just wage for the individual worker; but it should be applied with equal force to contracts made between nations: trade relations can no longer be based solely on the principle of free, unchecked competition, for it very often creates an economic dictatorship. Free trade can be called just only when it conforms to the demands of social justice. (no. 59)

ST. JOHN PAUL II

⟫ Writings and Teachings ⟪

Consumer Choices, Savings and Investments

It is . . . necessary to create lifestyles in which the quest for truth, beauty, goodness and communion with others . . . are the factors which determine consumer choices, savings and investments. . . . It is not a matter of the duty of charity alone, that is, the duty to give from one's "abundance," and sometimes even out of one's needs, in order to provide what is essential for the life of a poor person. I am referring to the fact that even the decision to invest in one place rather than another, in one productive sector rather than another, is always *a moral and cultural choice*. (Encyclical *Centesimus Annus* [*The Hundredth Year*], *On the Hundredth Anniversary of Rerum Novarum*, no. 37)

THE GOODNESS OF GOD'S GIFT

Life

"Life is always a good." (Encyclical *Evangelium Vitae* [*The Gospel of Life*], no. 34)

The Value of the Beauty of Nature and Its Prudent Cultivation

The aesthetic value of creation cannot be overlooked. Our very contact with nature has a deep restorative power; contemplation of its magnificence imparts peace and serenity. The Bible speaks again and again of the goodness and beauty of creation, which is called to glorify God (cf. Gn 1:4 ff; Ps 8:2; 104:1 ff; Wis 13:3-5; Sir 39:16, 33; 43:1, 9). More difficult perhaps, but no less profound, is the contemplation of the works of human ingenuity. Even cities can have a beauty all their own, one that ought to motivate people to care for their surroundings. Good urban planning is an important part of environmental protection, and respect for the natural contours of the land is an indispensable prerequisite for ecologically sound development. (Message for the 1990 World Day of Peace, no. 14)

THE MORAL ROOTS OF ENVIRONMENTAL PROBLEMS

Environmental Pollution Betrays Lack of Respect for Life

The most profound and serious indication of the moral implications underlying the ecological problem is the lack of *respect for life* evident in many of the patterns of environmental pollution. Often, the interests of production prevail over concern for the dignity of workers, while economic interests take priority over the good of individuals and even entire peoples. In these cases, pollution or environmental destruction is the result of an unnatural and reductionist vision which at times leads to a genuine contempt for man. (Message for the 1990 World Day of Peace, no. 7)

Respect for Human Life Affects Respect for Others and the Earth

The seriousness of the ecological issue lays bare the depth of man's moral crisis. If an appreciation of the value of the human person and of human life is lacking, we will also lose interest in others and in the earth itself. (Message for the 1990 World Day of Peace, no. 13)

Grave Responsibility to Preserve the Natural Order for Future Generations

Today the ecological crisis has assumed such proportions as to be the responsibility of everyone. . . . There is an order in the universe which must be respected, and that the human person, endowed with the capability of choosing freely, has a grave responsibility to preserve this order for the well-being of future generations. I wish to repeat that *the ecological crisis is a moral issue.* (Message for the 1990 World Day of Peace, no. 15)

ECOLOGICAL CONCERNS

Pollution Shows Lack of Respect for Life

The most profound and serious indication of the moral implications underlying the ecological problem is the lack of *respect for life* evident in many of the patterns of environmental pollution. Often, the interests of production prevail over concern for the dignity of workers, while economic interests take priority over the good of individuals and even entire peoples. In these cases, pollution or environmental destruction is the result of an unnatural and reductionist vision which at times leads to a genuine contempt for man. (Message for the 1990 World Day of Peace, no. 7)

Delicate Balance of Plant and Animal Life

Delicate ecological balances are upset by the uncontrolled destruction of animal and plant life or by a reckless exploitation of natural resources. It should be pointed out that all of this, even if carried out in the name of progress and well-being, is ultimately to mankind's disadvantage. (Message for the 1990 World Day of Peace, no. 7)

Genetic Manipulation of Animal and Plant Life

We can only look with deep concern at the enormous possibilities of biological research. We are not yet in a position to assess the biological disturbance that could result from indiscriminate genetic manipulation and from the unscrupulous development of new forms of plant and animal life, to say nothing of unacceptable experimentation regarding the origins of human life itself. (Message for the 1990 World Day of Peace, no. 7)

War and Ecological Damage

There is another dangerous menace which threatens us, namely *war*. Unfortunately, modern science already has the capacity to change the environment for hostile purposes. Alterations of this kind over the long term could have unforeseeable and still more serious consequences. Despite the international agreements which prohibit chemical, bacteriological and biological warfare, the fact is that laboratory research continues to develop new offensive weapons capable of altering the balance of nature.

Today, any form of war on a global scale would lead to incalculable ecological damage. But even local or regional wars, however limited, not only destroy human life and social structures, but also damage the land, ruining crops and vegetation as well as poisoning the soil and water. The survivors of war are forced to begin a new life in very difficult environmental conditions, which in turn create situations of extreme social unrest, with further negative consequences for the environment. (Message for the 1990 World Day of Peace, no. 12)

CONSEQUENCES OF SIN ON CREATION

Effects of Unrestrained Industrial Growth and Agricultural Development

Many recent [scientific and technological] discoveries have brought undeniable benefits to humanity. Indeed, they demonstrate the nobility of the human vocation to participate *responsibly* in God's creative action in the world. Unfortunately, it is now clear that the application of these discoveries in the fields of industry and agriculture have produced harmful long-term effects. This has led to the painful realization that *we cannot interfere in one area of the ecosystem without paying due attention both to the consequences of such interference in other areas and to the well-being of future generations.*

The gradual depletion of the ozone layer and the related "greenhouse effect" has now reached crisis proportions as a consequence of industrial growth, massive urban concentrations and vastly increased energy needs. Industrial waste, the burning of fossil fuels, unrestricted deforestation, the use of certain types of herbicides, coolants and propellants: all of these are known to harm the atmosphere and environment. The resulting meteorological and atmospheric changes range from damage to health to the possible future submersion of low-lying lands.

While in some cases the damage already done may well be irreversible, in many other cases it can still be halted. It is necessary, however, that the entire human community . . . take seriously the responsibility that is theirs. (Message for the 1990 World Day of Peace, no. 6)

Lack of Respect for Nature Threatens World Peace

World peace is threatened not only by the arms race, regional conflicts and continued injustices among peoples and nations, but also by a lack of *due respect for nature*, by the plundering of natural resources and by a progressive decline in the quality of life. The sense of precariousness and insecurity that such a situation engenders is a seedbed for collective selfishness, disregard for others and dishonesty. Faced with the widespread destruction of the environment, people everywhere are coming to understand that we cannot continue to use the goods of the earth as we have in the past. (Message for the 1990 World Day of Peace, no. 16)

THE PATH FORWARD: CONDUCT TOWARD CREATION

Obligation for Catholics to Care for Creation

I should like to address directly my brothers and sisters in the Catholic Church, in order to remind them of their serious obligation to care for all of creation. The commitment of believers to a healthy environment for everyone stems directly from their belief in God the Creator, from their recognition of the effects of original and personal sin, and from the certainty of having been redeemed by Christ. Respect for life and for the dignity of the human person extends also to the rest of creation, which is called to join man in praising God (cf. Ps 148:96). (Message for the 1990 World Day of Peace, no. 16)

Respect Life and Creation

Respect for life, and above all for the dignity of the human person, is the ultimate guiding norm for any sound economic, industrial or scientific progress.

The complexity of the ecological question is evident to all. There are, however, certain underlying principles, which, while respecting the legitimate autonomy and the specific competence of those involved, can direct research towards adequate and lasting solutions. These principles are essential to the building of a peaceful society; *no peaceful society can afford to neglect either respect for life or the fact that there is an integrity to creation.* (Message for the 1990 World Day of Peace, no. 7)

Honor the Created Order

Theology, philosophy and science all speak of a harmonious universe, of a "cosmos" endowed with its own integrity, its own internal, dynamic balance. *This order must be respected.* The human race is called to explore this order, to examine it with due care and to make use of it while safeguarding its integrity. (Message for the 1990 World Day of Peace, no. 8)

Share the Fruits of Creation

The earth is ultimately *a common heritage, the fruits of which are for the benefit of all.* In the words of the Second Vatican Council, "God destined the earth and all it contains for the use of every individual and all peoples" (*Gaudium et Spes*, 69). This has direct consequences for the problem at hand. It is manifestly unjust that a privileged few should continue to accumulate excess goods, squandering available resources, while masses of people are living in conditions of misery at the very lowest level of subsistence. Today, the dramatic threat of ecological breakdown is teaching us the extent to which greed and selfishness—both individual and collective—are contrary to the order of creation, an order which is characterized by mutual interdependence. (Message for the 1990 World Day of Peace, no. 8)

The Role of Governance to Protect the Atmosphere

In many cases the effects of ecological problems transcend the borders of individual States; hence their solution cannot be found solely on the national level. . . . The State should also actively endeavor within its own territory to prevent destruction of the atmosphere and biosphere, by carefully monitoring, among other things, the impact of new technological or scientific advances. The State also has the responsibility of ensuring that its citizens are not exposed to dangerous pollutants or toxic wastes. (Message for the 1990 World Day of Peace, no. 9)

Aid Economically Poor Countries

The proper ecological balance will not be found without *directly addressing the structural forms of poverty* that exist throughout the world. Rural poverty and unjust land distribution in many countries, for example, have led to subsistence farming and to the exhaustion of the soil. Once their land yields no more, many farmers move on to clear new land, thus accelerating uncontrolled deforestation, or they settle in urban centers which lack the infrastructure to receive them. Likewise, some heavily indebted countries are destroying their natural heritage, at the price of irreparable ecological imbalances, in order to develop new products for export. In the face of such situations it would be wrong to assign responsibility to the poor alone for the negative environmental consequences of their actions. Rather, the poor, to whom the earth is entrusted no less than to others, must be enabled to find a way out of their poverty. (Message for the 1990 World Day of Peace, no. 11)

Restrain Consumption: Simplicity, Moderation, Discipline

Modern society will find no solution to the ecological problem unless it *takes a serious look at its lifestyle.* In many parts of the world society is given to instant gratification and consumerism while remaining indifferent to the damage which these cause. . . . Simplicity, moderation and discipline, as well as a spirit of sacrifice, must become a part of everyday life, lest all suffer the negative consequences of the careless habits of a few. (Message for the 1990 World Day of Peace, no. 13)

Conversion of Mind and Action

A true education in responsibility entails a genuine conversion in ways of thought and behavior. Churches and religious bodies, nongovernmental and governmental organizations, indeed all members of society, have a precise role to play in such education. The first educator, however, is the family, where the child learns to respect his neighbor and to love nature. (Message for the 1990 World Day of Peace, no. 13)

The Path Forward: Use of Created Things

Responsibility Toward the Environment

"Man has a specific responsibility towards the environment in which he lives, towards the creation which God has put at the service of his personal dignity, of his life, not only for the present but also for future generations." (Evangelium Vitae, no. 42)

Biological and Moral Laws Govern the Natural World

It is the ecological question—ranging from the preservation of the natural habitats of the different species of animals and of other forms of life to "human ecology" properly speaking[28]—which finds in the Bible clear and strong ethical direction, leading to a solution which respects the great good of life, of every life. In fact, "the dominion granted to man by the Creator is not an absolute power, nor can one speak of a freedom to 'use and misuse', or to dispose of things as one pleases. The limitation imposed from the beginning by the Creator himself and expressed symbolically by the prohibition not to 'eat of the fruit of the tree' (cf. Gen 2:16-17) shows clearly enough that, when it comes to the natural world, we are subject not only to biological laws but also to moral ones, which cannot be violated with impunity."[29] (*Evangelium Vitae*, no. 42)

28   Cf. John Paul II, Encyclical Letter *Centesimus Annus* (May 1, 1991), no. 38.
29   John Paul II, Encyclical Letter *Sollicitudo Rei Socialis* (Dec. 30, 1987), no. 34.

POPE BENEDICT XVI

༄ Writings and Teachings ༄

GOD'S PLAN FOR CREATION

Jesus Is King of Israel, Universal King, and Lord of the Cosmos

We are celebrating the Solemnity of Christ the King . . . The title "King," designating Jesus, is very important in the Gospels . . . In this regard a progression can be noted: it starts with the expression "King of Israel" and extends to that of universal King, Lord of the cosmos and of history, thus exceeding by far the expectations of the Jewish people. It is yet again the mystery of Jesus Christ's death and Resurrection that lies at the heart of this process of the revelation of his kingship. (*Angelus*, St. Peter's Square, Nov. 22, 2009)

Jesus' Authority as King of the Universe Comes Through His Self-Offering

The Cross is the paradoxical sign of [Jesus'] kingship, which consists in the loving will of God the Father . . . It is in the very offering of himself in the sacrifice of expiation that Jesus becomes King of the universe, as he himself was to declare when he appeared to the Apostles after the Resurrection: "All authority in Heaven and on earth has been given to me" (Mt 28:18). (*Angelus*, St. Peter's Square, Nov. 22, 2009)

Nature Is Part of a Plan of Love and Truth

What we call "nature" in a cosmic sense has its origin in "a plan of love and truth" . . . The world "is not the product of any necessity whatsoever, nor of blind fate or chance . . . The world proceeds from the free will of God; he wanted to make his creatures share in his being, in his intelligence, and in his goodness" (*Catechism of the Catholic Church*, 295). The *Book of Genesis*, in its very first pages, points to the wise design of the cosmos: it comes forth from God's mind and finds its culmination in man and woman, made in the image and likeness of the Creator to "fill the earth" and to "have dominion over" it as "stewards" of God himself (cf. Gen 1:28). (Message for the 2010 World Day of Peace, no. 6)

Moral Roots of the Ecological Crisis

Preserving Creation Is Essential for Peace

Respect for creation is of immense consequence, not least because "creation is the beginning and the foundation of all God's works,"[1] and its preservation has now become essential for the pacific coexistence of mankind. Man's inhumanity to man has given rise to numerous threats to peace and to authentic and integral human development . . . Yet no less troubling are the threats arising from the neglect—if not downright misuse—of the earth and the natural goods that God has given us. For this reason, it is imperative that mankind renew and strengthen "that covenant between human beings and the environment, which should mirror the creative love of God, from whom we come and towards whom we are journeying."[2] (Message for the 2010 World Day of Peace, no. 1)

1   *Catechism of the Catholic Church*, no. 198.
2   Benedict XVI, Message for the 2008 World Day of Peace, no. 7.

The Human Relationship with and Obligations Toward the Environment

Integral human development is closely linked to the obligations which flow from *man's relationship with the natural environment*. The environment must be seen as God's gift to all people, and the use we make of it entails a shared responsibility for all humanity, especially the poor and future generations. (Message for the 2010 World Day of Peace, no. 2)

Caring for Gifts Received

Whenever nature, and human beings in particular, are seen merely as products of chance or an evolutionary determinism, our overall sense of responsibility wanes. On the other hand, seeing creation as God's gift to humanity helps us understand our vocation and worth as human beings. (Message for the 2010 World Day of Peace, no. 2)

Our Ecological Crisis Is Ultimately a Moral Crisis

The ecological crisis cannot be viewed in isolation from other related questions, since it is closely linked to the notion of development itself and our understanding of man in his relationship to others and to the rest of creation. Prudence would thus dictate a *profound, long-term review of our model of development* . . . The ecological health of the planet calls for this, but it is also demanded by the cultural and moral crisis of humanity whose symptoms have for some time been evident in every part of the world. Humanity needs a *profound cultural renewal* . . . Our present crises—be they economic, food-related, environmental or social—are ultimately also moral crises, and all of them are interrelated. (Message for the 2010 World Day of Peace, no. 5)

Disrupted Harmony with Creation and God

The harmony between the Creator, mankind and the created world, as described by Sacred Scripture, was disrupted by the sin of Adam and Eve . . . As a result, the work of "exercising dominion" over the earth, "tilling it and keeping it," was also disrupted, and conflict arose within and between mankind and the rest of creation (cf. Gen 3:17-19). Human beings let themselves be mastered by selfishness; they misunderstood the meaning of God's command and exploited creation out of a desire to exercise absolute domination over it. But the true meaning of God's original command, as the *Book of Genesis* clearly shows, was not a simple conferral of authority, but rather a summons to responsibility. (Message for the 2010 World Day of Peace, no. 6)

NEED FOR ACTION

Can We Remain Indifferent?

Can we remain indifferent before the problems associated with such realities as climate change, desertification, the deterioration and loss of productivity in vast agricultural areas, the pollution of rivers and aquifers, the loss of biodiversity, the increase of natural catastrophes and the deforestation of equatorial and tropical regions? Can we disregard the growing phenomenon of "environmental refugees," people who are forced by the degradation of their natural habitat to forsake it—and often their possessions as well—in order to face the dangers and uncertainties of forced displacement? Can we remain impassive in the face of actual and potential conflicts involving access to natural resources? All these are issues with a profound impact on the exercise of human rights, such as the right to life, food, health and development. (Message for the 2010 World Day of Peace, no. 4)

Nature Has an "Inbuilt Order"; The Wise Honor It

The wisdom of the ancients had recognized that nature is not at our disposal as "a heap of scattered refuse."[10] Biblical Revelation made us see that nature is a gift of the Creator, who gave it an inbuilt order and enabled man to draw from it the principles needed to "till it and keep it" (cf. Gen. 2:15).[11] Everything that exists belongs to God, who has entrusted it to man, albeit not for his arbitrary use. Once man, instead of acting as God's co-worker, sets himself up in place of God, he ends up provoking a rebellion on the part of nature, "which is more tyrannized than governed by him."[12] Man thus has a duty to exercise responsible stewardship over creation, to care for it and to cultivate it.[13] (Message for the 2010 World Day of Peace, no. 6)

10   Heraclitus of Ephesus (c. 535 – c. 475 B.C.), Fragment 22B124, in H. Diels-W. Kranz, Die Fragmente der Vorsokratiker, Weidmann, Berlin,1952, 6th ed.
11   Cf. Benedict XVI, Encyclical Letter *Caritas in Veritate*, no. 48.
12   John Paul II, Encyclical Letter *Centesimus Annus*, no. 37.
13   Cf. Benedict XVI, Encyclical Letter *Caritas in Veritate*, no. 50.

People Suffer When Others Neglect the Environment

Large numbers of people in different countries and areas of our planet are experiencing increased hardship because of the negligence or refusal of many others to exercise responsible stewardship over the environment. (Message for the 2010 World Day of Peace, no. 7)

POPE FRANCIS

✥ Writings and Teachings ✥

THE WISDOM OF CARING FOR CREATION

God Instructs Us to Care for Creation

Cultivating and caring for creation is an instruction of God which he gave not only at the beginning of history, but has also given to each one of us; it is part of his plan; it means making the world increase with responsibility, transforming it so that it may be a garden, an inhabitable place for us all. (General Audience, June 5, 2013)

Humanity Is Inseparable from the Natural Environment

We cannot say that mankind is here and *Creation*, the environment, is there. Ecology is total, it's human. . . . Man cannot be separated from the rest; there is a relationship which is reciprocally influential, both the environment on the person, and the person in a way which affects the environment; and the effect bounces back to man when the environment is mistreated. (Statement, "Workshop on Modern Slavery and Climate Change," July 21, 2015)

A Work of Mercy That Sustains Life

The Christian life involves the practice of the traditional seven corporal and seven spiritual works of mercy.[10] "We usually think of the works of mercy individually and in relation to a specific initiative: hospitals for the sick, soup kitchens for the hungry, shelters for the homeless, schools for those to be educated, the confessional and spiritual direction for those needing counsel and forgiveness . . . But if we look at the works of mercy as a whole, we see that the object of mercy is human life itself and everything it embraces."[11]

Obviously "human life itself and everything it embraces" includes care for our common home. So let me propose a complement to the two traditional sets of seven: may the works of mercy also include *care for our common home.*

As a spiritual work of mercy, care for our common home calls for a "grateful contemplation of God's world" (*Laudato Si'*, no. 214) which "allows us to discover in each thing a teaching which God wishes to hand on to us" (*ibid.*, no. 85). As a corporal work of mercy, care for our common home requires "simple daily gestures which break with the logic of violence, exploitation and selfishness" and "makes itself felt in every action that seeks to build a better world" (*ibid.*, nos. 230-31). (Message for the World Day of Prayer for the Care of Creation, Sept. 1, 2016)

10   The corporal works of mercy are feeding the hungry, giving drink to the thirsty, clothing the naked, welcoming the stranger, visiting the sick, visiting the imprisoned, burying the dead. The spiritual works of mercy are counselling the doubtful, instructing the ignorant, admonishing sinners, consoling the afflicted, forgiving offenses, bearing patiently those who do us ill, praying for the living and the dead.

11   Third Meditation, Retreat for the Jubilee for Priests, Rome, June 2, 2016.

How Do We Treat God's Gift?

God's gaze, at the beginning of the Bible, rests lovingly on his creation. From habitable land to life-giving waters, from fruit-bearing trees to animals that share our common home, everything is dear in the eyes of God, who offers creation to men and women as a precious gift to be preserved. (Message for the World Day of Prayer for the Care of Creation, Sept 1, 2019)

"Called to Be at the Heart of a Network of Life"

We have forgotten who we are: creatures made in the image of God (cf. Gen 1:27) and called to dwell as brothers and sisters in a common home. We were created not to be tyrants, but to be at the heart of a network of life made up of millions of species lovingly joined together for us by our Creator. Now is the time to rediscover our vocation as children of God, brothers and sisters, and stewards of creation. Now is the time to repent, to be converted and to return to our roots. We are beloved creatures of God, who in his goodness calls us to love life and live it in communion with the rest of creation. (Message for the World Day of Prayer for the Care of Creation, Sept 1, 2019)

MORAL ROOTS AND BRANCHES OF THE ECOLOGICAL CRISIS

Neglect of Creation Results When We Drift Away from God

We are losing our attitude of wonder, of contemplation, of listening to creation and thus we no longer manage to interpret in it what Benedict XVI calls "the rhythm of the love-story between God and man." Why does this happen? Why do we think and live horizontally, we have drifted away from God, we no longer read his signs. (General Audience, June 5, 2013)

When Money Has Dominion, Rather Than Men and Women

The popes have spoken of a *human ecology*, closely connected with *environmental ecology*. We are living in a time of crisis; we see it in the environment, but above all we see it in men and women. The human person is in danger: this much is certain . . . It is no longer man who commands, but money, money, cash commands. And God our Father gave us the task of protecting the earth—not for money, but for ourselves: for men and women. We have this task! Nevertheless men and women are sacrificed to the idols of profit and consumption: it is the "culture of waste." If a computer breaks it is a tragedy, but poverty, the needs and dramas of so many people end up being considered normal. If on a winter's night . . . for example—someone dies, that is not news. If there are children in so many parts of the world who have nothing to eat, that is not news, it seems normal. It cannot be so! (General Audience, June 5, 2013)

Material Waste and Disregard for Human Life

This "culture of waste" tends to become a common mentality that infects everyone. Human life, the person, are no longer seen as a primary value to be respected and safeguarded, especially if they are poor or disabled, if they are not yet useful—like the unborn child—or are no longer of any use—like the elderly person. This culture of waste has also made us insensitive to wasting and throwing out excess foodstuffs, which is especially condemnable when, in every part of the world, unfortunately, many people and families suffer hunger and malnutrition. There was a time when our grandparents were very careful not to throw away any left-over food. Consumerism has induced us to be accustomed to excess and to the daily waste of food, whose value, which goes far beyond mere financial parameters, we are no longer able to judge correctly. (General Audience, June 5, 2013)

Going to the Root: Recognize That Our Source and Ultimate Meaning Is in God

The first kind of indifference in human society is indifference to God, which then leads to indifference to one's neighbor and to the environment. . . . We have come to think that we are the source and creator of ourselves, our lives and society. We feel self-sufficient, prepared not only to find a substitute for God but to do completely without him. As a consequence, we feel that we owe nothing to anyone but ourselves, and we claim only rights.[4] Against this erroneous understanding of the person, Pope Benedict XVI observed that neither man himself nor human development can, on their own, answer the question of our ultimate meaning.[5] Paul VI likewise stated that "there is no true humanism but that which is open to the Absolute, and is conscious of a vocation which gives human life its authentic significance."[6] (Message for 2016 World Day of Peace, no. 3)

4   Cf. Benedict XVI, Encyclical Letter *Caritas in Veritate*, no. 43.
5   Cf. ibid., no. 16.
6   Encyclical *Populorum Progressio*, no. 42.

Intemperance and Ungodly Desires

Indeed, when we fail to live as children of God, we often behave in a destructive way towards our neighbors and other creatures—and ourselves as well—since we begin to think more or less consciously that we can use them as we will. Intemperance then takes the upper hand: we start to live a life that exceeds those limits imposed by our human condition and nature itself. We yield to those untrammeled desires that the Book of Wisdom sees as typical of the ungodly, those who act without thought for God or hope for the future (cf. 2:1-11). Unless we tend constantly towards Easter, towards the horizon of the Resurrection, the mentality expressed in the slogans *"I want it all and I want it now!"* and *"Too much is never enough,"* gains the upper hand. (Message for Lent 2019)

Sin Disrupts Communion with God, Others, and Creation

Sin . . . from its first appearance has disrupted our communion with God, with others and with creation itself, to which we are linked in a particular way by our body. This rupture of communion with God likewise undermines our harmonious relationship with the environment in which we are called to live, so that the garden has become a wilderness (cf. Gen 3:17-18). Sin leads man to consider himself the god of creation, to see himself as its absolute master and to use it, not for the purpose willed by the Creator but for his own interests, to the detriment of other creatures.

Once God's law, the law of love, is forsaken, then the law of the strong over the weak takes over. The sin that lurks in the human heart (cf. Mk 7:20-23) takes the shape of greed and unbridled pursuit of comfort, lack of concern for the good of others and even of oneself. It leads to the exploitation of creation, both persons and the environment, due to that insatiable covetousness which sees every desire as a right and sooner or later destroys all those in its grip. (Message for Lent 2019)

Neglectful Human Activity Degrades God's Gift of Creation

The human response to this gift [of creation] has been marked by sin, selfishness and a greedy desire to possess and exploit. Egoism and self-interest have turned creation, a place of encounter and sharing, into an arena of competition and conflict. In this way, the environment itself is endangered: something *good* in God's eyes has become something to be *exploited* in human hands. Deterioration has increased in recent decades: constant pollution, the continued use of fossil fuels, intensive agricultural exploitation and deforestation are causing global temperatures to rise above safe levels. The increase in the intensity and frequency of extreme weather phenomena and the desertification of the soil are causing immense hardship for the most vulnerable among us. Melting of glaciers, scarcity of water, neglect of water basins and the considerable presence of plastic and microplastics in the oceans are equally troubling, and testify to the urgent need for interventions that can no longer be postponed. (Message for the World Day of Prayer for the Care of Creation, Sept 1, 2019)

FORMS OF THE CRISIS

Food Waste

Let us remember well, however, that whenever food is thrown out it is as if it were stolen from the table of the poor, from the hungry! I ask everyone to reflect on the problem of the loss and waste of food, to identify ways and approaches which, by seriously dealing with this problem, convey solidarity and sharing with the underprivileged. (General Audience, June 5, 2013)

Poverty and Migration

One of the most notable things when the environment, when creation isn't looked after, is the unfettered growth of Cities. It is a worldwide phenomenon. It is as if the heads, the big cities, made themselves large, but each time with greater areas of poverty and misery, where the people suffer the effects of environmental neglect. The phenomenon of migration is included in this sense. Why do people come to the big cities, to the poverty belts of big cities—the shanty towns, slums and favelas? Why do they do this? It is simply because the rural world doesn't offer them opportunities. (Statement, "Workshop on Modern Slavery and Climate Change," July 21, 2015)

Agricultural Technicization and Rare Diseases

Health is at stake. The multitude of "rare diseases," as they are called, comes from many elements used to fertilize fields—or who knows, no one yet understands the cause—however they come from excessive technicization. (Statement, "Workshop on Modern Slavery and Climate Change," July 21, 2015)

Excess Technicization and Human Trafficking

What happens when all these phenomena of excessive techniciza-tion, without caring for the environment, in addition to natural phenomena, affect migration? Unemployment and then human trafficking. Illegal work, without contracts, working "under the table" is occurring more and more frequently. How it has increased! (Statement, "Workshop on Modern Slavery and Climate Change," July 21, 2015)

Technicization of Agriculture and Mining: Disease and Human Slavery

Illegal work is truly pervasive, and this means that people don't earn enough to live. This can lead to criminal behavior all the problems that occur in large cities due to these migrations caused by exces-sive technicization. I refer in particular to the agricultural environ-ment and also to human trafficking in the mining industry. Slavery in mines is a major issue. It involves the use of certain elements in the treatment of minerals—arsenic, cyanide which cause diseases in the population. There is a very great responsibility in this. It all bounces back, it all turns around, everything has a rebound affect against the person himself. It can include human trafficking for purposes of slave labor or prostitution—sources of work to enable survival today. (Statement, "Workshop on Modern Slavery and Climate Change," July 21, 2015)

Desertification and Deforestation

One of the greatest problems at issue relates to oxygen and water. Namely, the desertification of large areas through deforestation. Next to me is the Cardinal Archbishop representing the Brazilian Amazon, who can tell us what deforestation means today in the Amazon, which is the world's lungs. Congo and Amazonia are the world's great lungs. (Statement, "Workshop on Modern Slavery and Climate Change," July 21, 2015)

Indifference Toward the Environment Creates New Forms Poverty and Injustice

Indifference to the natural environment, by countenancing deforestation, pollution and natural catastrophes which uproot entire communities from their ecosystem and create profound insecurity, ends up creating new forms of poverty and new situations of injustice, often with dire consequences for security and peace. How many wars have been fought, and how many will continue to be fought, over a shortage of goods or out of an insatiable thirst for natural resources? (cf. Encyclical Letter *Laudato Si'*, nos. 31 and 48). (Message for 2016 World Day of Peace, no. 4)

Various Environmental Ills

Because we dwell in a common home, we cannot help but ask ourselves about the state of its health, as I sought to do in *Laudato Si'*. Water and air pollution, the indiscriminate exploitation of forests and the destruction of the natural environment are often the result of man's indifference to man, since everything is interrelated. Then too, there is the way we treat animals, which has an effect on the way we treat other people, and the cases where people freely do elsewhere what they would never dare do at home. (Message for 2016 World Day of Peace, no. 3)

Loss of the Diversity of Animal Life

We must not be indifferent or resigned to the loss of biodiversity and the destruction of ecosystems, often caused by our irresponsible and selfish behavior. "Because of us, thousands of species will no longer give glory to God by their very existence, nor convey their message to us. We have no such right" (*Laudato Si'*, no. 33). (Message for the World Day of Prayer for the Care of Creation, Sept. 1, 2016)

Global Warming and Climate Change

Global warming continues, due in part to human activity: 2015 was the warmest year on record, and 2016 will likely be warmer still. This is leading to ever more severe droughts, floods, fires and extreme weather events. Climate change is also contributing to the heart-rending refugee crisis. The world's poor, though least responsible for climate change, are most vulnerable and already suffering its impact. (Message for the World Day of Prayer for the Care of Creation, Sept. 1, 2016)

Need for Clean, Accessible Drinking Water

I would like to draw attention to the question of *water*. It is a very simple and precious element, yet access to it is, sadly, for many people difficult if not impossible. Nonetheless, "access to safe drinkable water is a basic and universal human right, since it is essential to human survival and, as such, is a condition for the exercise of other human rights. Our world owes a great social debt towards the poor who lack access to drinking water, because they are denied the right to a life consistent with their inalienable dignity" (*Laudato Si'*, no. 30). . . .

In considering the fundamental role of water in creation and in human development, I feel the need to give thanks to God for "Sister Water," simple and useful for life like nothing else on our planet. Precisely for this reason, care for water sources and water basins is an urgent imperative. Today, more than ever, we need to look beyond immediate concerns (cf. *Laudato Si'*, no. 36) and beyond a purely utilitarian view of reality, "in which efficiency and productivity are entirely geared to our individual benefit" (ibid., no. 159). We urgently need shared projects and concrete gestures that recognize that every privatization of the natural good of water, at the expense of the human right to have access to this good, is unacceptable. (Message for the World Day of Prayer for the Care of Creation, Sept. 1, 2018)

Failure to Protect Rivers, Seas, and Oceans

I would like also to mention the issue of the seas and oceans. It is our duty to thank the Creator for the impressive and marvelous gift of the great waters and all that they contain (cf. Gen 1:20-21; Ps 146:6), and to praise him for covering the earth with the oceans (cf. Ps 104:6). To ponder the immense open seas and their incessant movement can also represent an opportunity to turn our thoughts to God, who constantly accompanies his creation, guiding its course and sustaining its existence (cf. St. John Paul II, Catechesis, May 7, 1986).

Constant care for this inestimable treasure represents today an ineluctable duty and a genuine challenge. There is need for an effective cooperation between men and women of good will in assisting the ongoing work of the Creator. Sadly, all too many efforts fail due to the lack of effective regulation and means of control, particularly with regard to the protection of marine areas beyond national confines (cf. *Laudato Si'*, no. 174). We cannot allow our seas and oceans to be littered by endless fields of floating plastic. Here too, our active commitment is needed to confront this emergency. . . .

It is my prayerful hope that Christian communities may contribute more and more concretely helping everyone to enjoy this indispensable resource, in respectful care for the gifts received from the Creator, and in particular rivers, seas and oceans. (Message for the World Day of Prayer for the Care of Creation, Sept. 1, 2018)

A CALL FOR REPENTANCE AND CONVERSION

There Is Always Hope—With God, We Can Attain Peace

God is not indifferent! God cares about mankind! God does not abandon us! . . . Peace is both God's gift and a human achievement. As a gift of God, it is entrusted to all men and women, who are called to attain it. (Message for 2016 World Day of Peace, no. 1)

Learn to Give and Forgive

I want to invite the Church to pray and work so that every Christian will have a humble and compassionate heart, one capable of proclaiming and witnessing to mercy. It is my hope that all of us will learn to "forgive and give," to become more open "to those living on the outermost fringes of society—fringes which modern society itself creates." (Message for 2016 World Day of Peace, no. 2)

Capacity to Work for the Common Good

There are many good reasons to believe in mankind's capacity to act together in solidarity and, on the basis of our interconnection and interdependence, to demonstrate concern for the more vulnerable of our brothers and sisters and for the protection of the common good. This attitude of mutual responsibility is rooted in our fundamental vocation to fraternity and a life in common. Personal dignity and interpersonal relationships are what constitute us as human beings whom God willed to create in his own image and likeness. As creatures endowed with inalienable dignity, we are related to all our brothers and sisters, for whom we are responsible and with whom we act in solidarity. (Message for 2016 World Day of Peace, no. 2)

To Overuse, or Under Care for . . . Is to Sin

God gave us the earth "to till and to keep" (Gen 2:15) in a balanced and respectful way. To till too much, to keep too little, is to sin. (Message for the World Day of Prayer for the Care of Creation, Sept. 1, 2016)

Sins Against Ourselves, Sins Against God

My brother, Ecumenical Patriarch Bartholomew has courageously and prophetically continued to point out our sins against creation. "For human beings . . . to destroy the biological diversity of God's creation; for human beings to degrade the integrity of the earth by causing changes in its climate, by stripping the earth of its natural forests or destroying its wetlands; for human beings to contaminate the earth's waters, its land, its air, and its life—these are sins." Further, "to commit a crime against the natural world is a sin against ourselves and a sin against God."[2] (Message for the World Day of Prayer for the Care of Creation, Sept. 1, 2016)

2   Patriarch Bartholomew, Address in Santa Barbara, California (Nov. 8, 1997).

Examining One's Conscience Before God

The first step in this process is always an examination of conscience, which involves "gratitude and gratuitousness, a recognition that the world is God's loving gift, and that we are called quietly to imitate his generosity in self-sacrifice and good works . . . It also entails a loving awareness that we are not disconnected from the rest of creatures, but joined in a splendid universal communion.

As believers, we do not look at the world from without but from within, conscious of the bonds with which the Father has linked us to all beings" (*Laudato Si'*, no. 220).

Turning to this bountiful and merciful Father who awaits the return of each of his children, we can acknowledge our sins against creation, the poor and future generations. "Inasmuch as we all generate small ecological damage," we are called to acknowledge "our contribution, smaller or greater, to the disfigurement and destruction of creation."[3] This is the first step on the path of conversion. . . .

Let us repent of the harm we are doing to our common home. After a serious examination of conscience and moved by sincere repentance, we can confess our sins against the Creator, against creation, and against our brothers and sisters. (Message for the World Day of Prayer for the Care of Creation, Sept. 1, 2016)

3   Patriarch Bartholomew, Message for the Day of Prayer for the Protection of Creation (Sept.1, 2012).

Practical Changes to One's Daily Habits: No Effort Is Too Small

Examining our consciences, repentance and confession to our Father who is rich in mercy lead to a firm purpose of amendment. This in turn must translate into concrete ways of thinking and acting that are more respectful of creation. For example: "avoiding the use of plastic and paper, reducing water consumption, separating refuse, cooking only what can reasonably be consumed, showing care for other living beings, using public transport or car-pooling, planting trees, turning off unnecessary lights, or any number of other practices" (*Laudato Si'*, no. 211). We must not think that these efforts are too small to improve our world. (Message for the World Day of Prayer for the Care of Creation, Sept. 1, 2016)

A Question to Focus Our Resolve

A single question can keep our eyes fixed on the goal: "What kind of world do we want to leave to those who come after us, to children who are now growing up?" (*Laudato Si'*, no. 160). (Message for the World Day of Prayer for the Care of Creation, Sept. 1, 2016)

Implore God's Mercy for Sins Against Creation

Let us learn to implore God's mercy for those sins against creation that we have not hitherto acknowledged and confessed. Let us likewise commit ourselves to taking concrete steps towards ecological conversion, which requires a clear recognition of our responsibility to ourselves, our neighbors, creation and the Creator (*Laudato Si'*, nos. 10 and 229). (Message for the World Day of Prayer for the Care of Creation, Sept. 1, 2016)

The Spiritual Life Cannot Be Separated from Material Realities

We need always to keep in mind that, for believers in Jesus Christ, the Word of God who became man for our sake, "the life of the spirit is not dissociated from the body or from nature or from worldly realities, but lived in and with them, in communion with all that surrounds us" (*Laudato Si'*, no. 216). The ecological crisis thus summons us to a profound spiritual conversion: Christians are called to "an ecological conversion whereby the effects of their encounter with Jesus Christ become evident in their relationship with the world around them" (ibid., no. 217). For "living our vocation to be protectors of God's handiwork is essential to a life of virtue" (ibid.). (Letter on the World Day of Prayer for the Care of Creation, Sept. 1, 2015)

Day of Prayer to Ask God's Pardon for Sins Against Creation

The annual World Day of Prayer for the Care of Creation will offer individual believers and communities a fitting opportunity to reaffirm their personal vocation to be stewards of creation, to thank God for the wonderful handiwork which he has entrusted to our care, and to implore his help for the protection of creation as well as his pardon for the sins committed against the world in which we live. (Letter on the World Day of Prayer for the Care of Creation, Sept. 1, 2015)

Creation Longs for True Children of God

Creation urgently needs the revelation of the children of God, who have been made "a new creation." For "if anyone is in Christ, he is a new creation; the old has passed away; behold, the new has come" (2 Cor 5:17). Indeed, by virtue of their being revealed, *creation itself can celebrate a Pasch*, opening itself to a new heaven and a new earth (cf. Rev 21:1). The path to Easter demands that we renew our faces and hearts as Christians through repentance, conversion and forgiveness, so as to live fully the abundant grace of the paschal mystery.

This "eager longing," this expectation of all creation, will be fulfilled in the revelation of the children of God, that is, when Christians and all people enter decisively into the "travail" that conversion entails. All creation is called, with us, to go forth "from its bondage to decay and obtain the glorious liberty of the children of God" (Rom 8:21). (Message for Lent 2019)

Sacrificial Love, Surrender to God, and Charity Bring Joy

Fasting, that is, learning to change our attitude towards others and all of creation, turning away from the temptation to "devour" everything to satisfy our voracity and being ready to suffer for love, which can fill the emptiness of our hearts. *Prayer*, which teaches us to abandon idolatry and the self-sufficiency of our ego, and to acknowledge our need of the Lord and his mercy. *Almsgiving*, whereby we escape from the insanity of hoarding everything for ourselves in the illusory belief that we can secure a future that does not belong to us. And thus to rediscover the joy of God's plan for creation and for each of us, which is to love him, our brothers and sisters, and the entire world, and to find in this love our true happiness. (Message for Lent 2019)

Christ's Victory Over Sin and Death Transforms All Creation

[The] forty days spent by the Son of God in the *desert* of creation had the goal of making it once more that *garden* of communion with God that it was before original sin (cf. Mk 1:12-13; Is 51:3). May our Lent this year be a journey along that same path, bringing the hope of Christ also to creation, so that it may be "set free from its bondage to decay and obtain the glorious liberty of the children of God" (Rom 8:21). Let us not allow this season of grace to pass in vain! Let us ask God to help us set out on a path of true conversion. Let us leave behind our selfishness and self-absorption, and turn to Jesus' Pasch. Let us stand beside our brothers and sisters in need, sharing our spiritual and material goods with them. In this way, by concretely welcoming Christ's victory over sin and death into our lives, we will also radiate its transforming power to all of creation. (Message for Lent 2019)

⭑ Encyclical *Laudato Si'* ⭑ (*On Care for Our Common Home*)

SIN AFFECTS CREATION

The Violence in Our Hearts Manifests in the Soil, Water, and Air

"Praise be to you, my Lord, through our Sister, Mother Earth, who sustains and governs us, and who produces various fruit with colored flowers and herbs."[1] This sister now cries out to us because of the harm we have inflicted on her by our irresponsible use and abuse of the goods with which God has endowed her. We have come to see ourselves as her lords and masters, entitled to plunder her at will. The violence present in our hearts, wounded by sin, is also reflected in the symptoms of sickness evident in the soil, in the water, in the air and in all forms of life. (nos. 1-2)

---

1   *Canticle of the Creatures*, in *Francis of Assisi: Early Documents*, vol. 1, New York-London-Manila, 1999, 113-114.

Repentance Needed for Damage Caused to Creation

The beloved Ecumenical Patriarch Bartholomew, with whom we share the hope of full ecclesial communion . . . has spoken in particular of the need for each of us to repent of the ways we have harmed the planet, for "inasmuch as we all generate small ecological damage", we are called to acknowledge "our contribution, smaller or greater, to the disfigurement and destruction of creation."[14] He has repeatedly stated this firmly and persuasively, challenging us to acknowledge our sins against creation: "For human beings . . . to destroy the biological diversity of God's creation; for human beings to degrade the integrity of the earth by causing changes in its climate, by stripping the earth of its natural forests or destroying its wetlands; for human beings to contaminate the earth's waters, its land, its air, and its life—these are sins."[15] For "to commit a crime against the natural world is a sin against ourselves and a sin against God."[16] (nos. 7-8)

14   Patriarch Bartholomew, Message for the Day of Prayer for the Protection of Creation (Sept. 1, 2012).
15   Patriarch Bartholomew, Address, Santa Barbara, California (Nov. 8, 1997); cf. John Chryssavgis, *On Earth as in Heaven: Ecological Vision and Initiatives of Ecumenical Patriarch Bartholomew*, Bronx, New York, 2012.
16   Ibid.

Industrial Pollution Harms Human Health

Account must also be taken of the pollution produced by residue, including dangerous waste present in different areas. Each year hundreds of millions of tons of waste are generated, much of it non-biodegradable, highly toxic and radioactive, from homes and businesses, from construction and demolition sites, from clinical, electronic and industrial sources. . . . Industrial waste and chemical products utilized in cities and agricultural areas can lead to bioaccumulation in the organisms of the local population, even when levels of toxins in those places are low. Frequently no measures are taken until after people's health has been irreversibly affected. (no. 21)

Effects of Climate Change on the Poor

Climate change is a global problem with grave implications: environmental, social, economic, political and for the distribution of goods. . . . Many of the poor live in areas particularly affected by phenomena related to warming, and their means of subsistence are largely dependent on natural reserves and ecosystemic services such as agriculture, fishing and forestry. . . . For example, changes in climate, to which animals and plants cannot adapt, lead them to migrate; this in turn affects the livelihood of the poor, who are then forced to leave their homes, with great uncertainty for their future and that of their children. There has been a tragic rise in the number of migrants seeking to flee from the growing poverty caused by environmental degradation. (no. 25)

Attacks on Nature Are Sin

Sin is manifest in all its destructive power in wars, the various forms of violence and abuse, the abandonment of the most vulnerable, and attacks on nature. (no. 66)

IT IS GOD'S CREATION

God's Love Gives Life to All Creation

Creation is of the order of love. God's love is the fundamental moving force in all created things: "For you love all things that exist, and detest none of the things that you have made; for you would not have made anything if you had hated it" (Wis 11:24). Every creature is thus the object of the Father's tenderness, who gives it its place in the world. Even the fleeting life of the least of beings is the object of his love, and in its few seconds of existence, God enfolds it with his affection. (no. 77)

"Creation," Which Is a Gift, Not Nature

Nature is usually seen as a system which can be studied, understood and controlled, whereas creation can only be understood as a gift from the outstretched hand of the Father of all, and as a reality illuminated by the love which calls us together into universal communion. (no. 76)

God's Art

The Spirit of God has filled the universe . . . "Nature is nothing other than a certain kind of art, namely God's art, impressed upon things . . . It is as if a shipbuilder were able to give timbers the wherewithal to move themselves to take the form of a ship."[52] (no. 80)

52   Thomas Aquinas, *In octo libros Physicorum Aristotelis expositio*, Lib. II, lectio 14.

We Are Part of Creation, Called to Relationship with God

Human beings, even if we postulate a process of evolution, also possess a uniqueness which cannot be fully explained by the evolution of other open systems. Each of us has his or her own personal identity and is capable of entering into dialogue with others and with God himself. Our capacity to reason, to develop arguments, to be inventive, to interpret reality and to create art, along with other not yet discovered capacities, are signs of a uniqueness which transcends the spheres of physics and biology. The sheer novelty involved in the emergence of a personal being within a material universe presupposes a direct action of God and a particular call to life and to relationship on the part of a "Thou" who addresses himself to another "thou." The biblical accounts of creation invite us to see each human being as a subject who can never be reduced to the status of an object. (no. 81)

Right Dominion and Stewardship

Dominion, Not Domination

The earth was here before us and it has been given to us. This allows us to respond to the charge that Judeo-Christian thinking, on the basis of the Genesis account which grants man "dominion" over the earth (cf. Gen 1:28), has encouraged the unbridled exploitation of nature by painting him as domineering and destructive by nature. This is not a correct interpretation of the Bible as understood by the Church. Although it is true that we Christians have at times incorrectly interpreted the Scriptures, nowadays we must forcefully reject the notion that our being created in God's image and given dominion over the earth justifies absolute domination over other creatures. (no. 67)

The Earth Is the Lord's

"The earth is the Lord's" (Ps 24:1); to him belongs "the earth with all that is within it" (Dt 10:14). Thus God rejects every claim to absolute ownership: "The land shall not be sold in perpetuity, for the land is mine; for you are strangers and sojourners with me" (Lev 25:23). (no. 67)

Creatures Are More Than Just an Economic Resource

It would also be mistaken to view other living beings as mere objects subjected to arbitrary human domination. When nature is viewed solely as a source of profit and gain, this has serious consequences for society. This vision of "might is right" has engendered immense inequality, injustice and acts of violence against the majority of humanity, since resources end up in the hands of the first comer or the most powerful: the winner takes all. Completely at odds with this model are the ideals of harmony, justice, fraternity and peace as proposed by Jesus. As he said of the powers of his own age: "You know that the rulers of the Gentiles lord it over them, and their great men exercise authority over them. It shall not be so among you; but whoever would be great among you must be your servant" (Mt 20:25-26). (no. 82)

Conversion of Heart and Mind

Sacrifice, Generosity, Sharing, Asceticism

[Patriarch] Bartholomew has drawn attention to the ethical and spiritual roots of environmental problems, which require that we look for solutions not only in technology but in a change of humanity; otherwise we would be dealing merely with symptoms. He asks us to replace consumption with sacrifice, greed with generosity, wastefulness with a spirit of sharing, an asceticism which "entails learning to give, and not simply to give up. It is a way of loving, of moving gradually away from what I want to what God's world needs."[17] (no. 9)

17   Lecture at the Monastery of Utstein, Norway (June 23, 2003).

Reconciliation Between God, Humanity, and Creation

The creation accounts in the book of Genesis contain, in their own symbolic and narrative language, profound teachings about human existence and its historical reality. They suggest that human life is grounded in three fundamental and closely intertwined relationships: with God, with our neighbor and with the earth itself. According to the Bible, these three vital relationships have been broken, both outwardly and within us. This rupture is sin. The harmony between the Creator, humanity and creation as a whole was disrupted by our presuming to take the place of God and refusing to acknowledge our creaturely limitations. This in turn distorted our mandate to "have dominion" over the earth (cf. Gn 1:28), to "till it and keep it" (Gn 2:15). As a result, the originally harmonious relationship between human beings and nature became conflictual (cf. Gn 3:17-19). It is significant that the harmony which Saint Francis of Assisi experienced with all creatures was seen as a healing of that rupture. Saint Bonaventure held that, through universal reconciliation with every creature, Saint Francis in some way returned to the state of original innocence.[40] (no. 66)

40   Cf. Bonaventure, *The Major Legend of Saint Francis*, VIII, 1, in *Francis of Assisi: Early Documents*, vol. 2, New York-London-Manila, 2000, 586.

A Path Forward

A Conversation That Includes Everyone

I urgently appeal, then, for a new dialogue about how we are shaping the future of our planet. We need a conversation which includes everyone, since the environmental challenge we are undergoing, and its human roots, concern and affect us all. (no. 14)

Establishing New Consumer Habits

An awareness of the gravity of today's cultural and ecological crisis must be translated into new habits. Many people know that our current progress and the mere amassing of things and pleasures are not enough to give meaning and joy to the human heart, yet they feel unable to give up what the market sets before them. In those countries which should be making the greatest changes in consumer habits, young people have a new ecological sensitivity and a generous spirit, and some of them are making admirable efforts to protect the environment. (no. 209)

Ecological Education at Home, School,

Ecological education can take place in a variety of settings: at school, in families, in the media, in catechesis and elsewhere. Good education plants seeds when we are young, and these continue to bear fruit throughout life. (no. 213)

TEACHINGS OF THE ROMAN CURIA

>>> *Compendium of the Social Doctrine of the Church* <<<
(Pontifical Council for Justice and Peace)

MORAL FOUNDATIONS FOR ADDRESSING THE ECOLOGICAL CRISIS

We Are a New Creation in Christ

Christ's disciple adheres, in faith and through the sacraments, to Jesus' Paschal Mystery, so that his *old self*, with its evil inclinations, is crucified with Christ. As a new creation he is then enabled by grace to "walk in newness of life" (Rom 6:4). (no. 40)

A Relationship with Created Things, Purified by the Cross

The relationship with the created universe and human activity aimed at tending it and transforming it, activity which is daily endangered by man's pride and his inordinate self-love, must be purified and perfected by the cross and resurrection of Christ. "Redeemed by Christ and made a new creature by the Holy Spirit, man can, indeed he must, love the things of God's creation: it is from God that he has received them, and it is as flowing from God's hand that he looks upon them and reveres them" (Second Vatican Ecumenical Council, Pastoral Constitution *Gaudium et Spes*, no. 37). (no. 44)

Sin Is Present in Creation, But Salvation Is Present in Jesus Christ

The doctrine of original sin, which teaches the universality of sin, has an important foundation: "If we say we have no sin, we deceive ourselves, and the truth is not in us" (1 Jn 1:8). This doctrine encourages men and women not to remain in guilt and not to take guilt lightly, continuously seeking scapegoats in other people and justification in the environment, in heredity, in institutions, in structures and in relationships. This is a teaching that unmasks such deceptions.

The doctrine of the universality of sin, however, must not be separated from the consciousness of the universality of salvation in Jesus Christ. If it is so separated it engenders a false anxiety of sin and a pessimistic view of the world and life, which leads to contempt of the cultural and civil accomplishments of mankind. (no. 120)

THE ENVIRONMENT IS A COLLECTIVE GOOD

Use of Animals, Plants, and the Natural Elements

Care for the environment represents a challenge for all of humanity. It is a matter of a common and universal duty, that of respecting a common good,[979] destined for all, by preventing anyone from using "with impunity the different categories of beings, whether living or inanimate—animals, plants, the natural elements—simply as one wishes, according to one's own economic needs."[980] It is a responsibility that must mature . . . all beings are interdependent in the universal order established by the Creator. "One must take into account the nature of each being and of its mutual connection in an ordered system, which is precisely the 'cosmos.' "[981] (no. 466)

979   Cf. John Paul II, Encyclical Letter *Centesimus Annus*, no. 40: AAS 83 (1991), 843.
980   John Paul II, Encyclical Letter *Sollicitudo Rei Socialis*, no. 34.
981   John Paul II, Encyclical Letter *Sollicitudo Rei Socialis*, no. 34.

Preserve Biodiversity Such as Exists in the Amazon Region

The environmental value of biodiversity . . . must be handled with a sense of responsibility and adequately protected, because it constitutes an extraordinary richness for all of humanity. In this regard, each person can easily recognize, for example, the importance of the Amazon, "one of the world's most precious natural regions because of its biodiversity which makes it vital for the environmental balance of the entire planet."[982] *Forests* help maintain the essential natural balance necessary for life.[983] Their destruction also through the inconsiderate and malicious setting of fires, accelerates the processes of desertification with risky consequences for water reserves and compromises the lives of many indigenous peoples and the well-being of future generations. (no. 466)

982   John Paul II, Apostolic Exhortation *Ecclesia in America*, no. 25.
983   Cf. John Paul II, Homily in Val Visdende (Italy) for the votive feast of St. John Gualberto (July 12, 1987).

Our Responsibility of Care Toward Those Who Come After Us

Responsibility for the environment, the common heritage of mankind, extends not only to present needs but also to those of the future. "We have inherited from past generations, and we have benefited from the work of our contemporaries: for this reason we have obligations towards all, and we cannot refuse to interest ourselves in those who will come after us, to enlarge the human family."[984] This is a responsibility that present generations have towards those of the future. (no. 467)

984   Paul VI, Encyclical Letter *Populorum Progressio*, 17.

Economic Development Should Respect the "Cycles of Nature"

Programs of economic development must carefully consider "the need to respect the integrity and the cycles of nature"[989] because natural resources are limited and some are not renewable. The present rhythm of exploitation is seriously compromising the availability of some natural resources for both the present and the future.[990] (no. 470)

990   John Paul II, Encyclical Letter *Sollicitudo Rei Socialis*, no. 26.
990   Cf. John Paul II, Encyclical Letter *Sollicitudo Rei Socialis*, no. 34.

Human Activity and Climate Change

Relations between human activity and climate change . . . given their extreme complexity, must be opportunely and constantly monitored at the scientific, political and juridical, national and international levels. The climate is a good that must be protected and reminds consumers and those engaged in industrial activity to develop a greater sense of responsibility for their behavior.[992] (no. 470)

992   Cf. John Paul II, Address to a study group of the Pontifical Academy of Sciences (Nov. 6, 1987).

Proactively Seek Environmental Protections

An economy respectful of the environment will not have the maximization of profits as its only objective, because environmental protection cannot be assured solely on the basis of financial calculations of costs and benefits. The environment is one of those goods that cannot be adequately safeguarded or promoted by market forces. . . . Seeking innovative ways to reduce the environmental impact of production and consumption of goods should be effectively encouraged. (no. 470)

ᔥ Excerpts from the ᕬ
Catechism of the Catholic Church

THE LAWS OF CREATION

Respect the Goodness of Every Creature

Each creature possesses its own particular goodness and perfection. For each one of the works of the "six days" it is said: "And God saw that it was good." "By the very nature of creation, material being is endowed with its own stability, truth and excellence, its own order and laws" (GS 36 § 1). Each of the various creatures, willed in its own being, reflects in its own way a ray of God's infinite wisdom and goodness. Man must therefore respect the particular goodness of every creature, to avoid any disordered use of things which would be in contempt of the Creator and would bring disastrous consequences for human beings and their environment. (no. 339)

All Creatures Are Interdependent

God wills the interdependence of creatures. The sun and the moon, the cedar and the little flower, the eagle and the sparrow: the spectacle of their countless diversities and inequalities tells us that no creature is self-sufficient. Creatures exist only in dependence on each other, to complete each other, in the service of each other. (no. 340)

Knowing the Laws of Nature

The *beauty of the universe*: The order and harmony of the created world results from the diversity of beings and from the relationships which exist among them. Man discovers them progressively as the laws of nature. They call forth the admiration of scholars.

The beauty of creation reflects the infinite beauty of the Creator and ought to inspire the respect and submission of man's intellect and will. (no. 341)

Respect the Laws Written into Creation by God

In creation God laid a foundation and established laws that remain firm, on which the believer can rely with confidence, for they are the sign and pledge of the unshakeable faithfulness of God's covenant.[214] For his part man must remain faithful to this foundation, and respect the laws which the Creator has written into it. (no. 346)

214   Cf. Heb 4:3-4; Jer 31:35-37; 33:19-26.

Respect for the Laws of Creation Is a Foundation for Morality

Respect for laws inscribed in creation and the relations which derive from the nature of things is a principle of wisdom and a foundation for morality. (no. 354)

We Are Subject to the Laws of Creation

Man is dependent on his Creator, and subject to the laws of creation and to the moral norms that govern the use of freedom. (no. 396)

CREATION IN GOD'S PLAN OF REDEMPTION

God's Good Plan for All Creation

In the Symbol of the faith the Church confesses the mystery of the Holy Trinity and of the plan of God's "good pleasure" for all creation: the Father accomplishes the "mystery of his will" by giving his beloved Son and his Holy Spirit for the salvation of the world and for the glory of his name (Eph 1:9). (no. 1066)

All Creation Is Offered to the Father in the Eucharistic Sacrifice

"In the Eucharistic sacrifice the whole of creation loved by God is presented to the Father through the death and the Resurrection of Christ. Through Christ the Church can offer the sacrifice of praise in thanksgiving for all that God has made good, beautiful, and just in creation and in humanity." (no. 1359)

The Praise of All Creation Is Offered to the God Through the Eucharistic Sacrifice

"The Eucharist is also the sacrifice of praise by which the Church sings the glory of God in the name of all creation. This sacrifice of praise is possible only through Christ: he unites the faithful to his person, to his praise, and to his intercession, so that the sacrifice of praise to the Father is offered *through* Christ and *with* him, to be accepted *in* him." (no. 1361)

Excerpts from the *Compendium of the Catechism of the Catholic Church*

TEACHINGS ON CREATION

What is the importance of affirming "In the beginning God created the heavens and the earth" (Gn 1:1)? The significance is that creation is the foundation of all God's saving plans. It shows forth the almighty and wise love of God, and it is the first step toward the covenant of the one God with his people. It is the beginning of the history of salvation which culminates in Christ; and it is the first answer to our fundamental questions regarding our very origin and destiny. (no. 51)

Who created the world? The Father, the Son, and the Holy Spirit are the one and indivisible principle of creation even though the work of creating the world is particularly attributed to God the Father. (no. 52)

Why was the world created? The world was created for the glory of God who wished to show forth and communicate his goodness, truth and beauty. The ultimate end of creation is that God, in Christ, might be "all in all" (1 Cor 15:28) for his glory and for our happiness. (no. 53)

How did God create the universe? God created the universe freely with wisdom and love. The world is not the result of any necessity, nor of blind fate, nor of chance. God created "out of nothing" (*ex nihilo*) (2 Mc 7:28) a world which is ordered and good and which he infinitely transcends. God preserves his creation in being and sustains it, giving it the capacity to act and leading it toward its fulfillment through his Son and the Holy Spirit. (no. 54)

GOD'S PURPOSES IN CREATION

What does Sacred Scripture teach about the creation of the visible world? Through the account of the "six days" of creation Sacred Scripture teaches us the value of the created world and its purpose, namely, to praise God and to serve humanity. Every single thing owes its very existence to God from whom it receives its goodness and perfection, its proper laws and its proper place in the universe. (no. 62)

What is the place of the human person in creation? The human person is the summit of visible creation in as much as he or she is created in the image and likeness of God. (no. 63)

What kind of bond exists between created things? There exist an interdependence and a hierarchy among creatures as willed by God. At the same time, there is also a unity and solidarity among creatures since all have the same Creator, are loved by him and are ordered to his glory. Respecting the laws inscribed in creation and the relations which derive from the nature of things is, therefore, a principle of wisdom and a foundation for morality. (no. 64)

What is the relationship between the work of creation and the work of redemption? The work of creation culminates in the still greater work of redemption, which in fact gives rise to a new creation in which everything will recover its true meaning and fulfillment. (no. 65)

In what sense do we understand man and woman as created "in the image of God"? The human person is created in the image of God in the sense that he or she is capable of knowing and of loving their Creator in freedom. Human beings are the only creatures on earth that God has willed for their own sake and has called to share, through knowledge and love, in his own divine life. All human beings, in as much as they are created in the image of God, have the dignity of a person. A person is not something but someone, capable of self-knowledge and of freely giving himself and entering into communion with God and with other persons. (no. 66)

For what purpose did God create man and woman? God has created everything for them; but he has created them to know, serve and love God, to offer all of creation in this world in thanksgiving back to him and to be raised up to life with him in heaven. Only in the mystery of the incarnate Word does the mystery of the human person come into true light. Man and woman are predestined to reproduce the image of the Son of God made Man, who is the perfect "image of the invisible God" (Colossians 1:15). (no. 67)

Why does the human race form a unity? All people form the unity of the human race by reason of the common origin which they have from God. God has made "from one ancestor all the nations of men" (Acts 17:26). All have but one Savior and are called to share in the eternal happiness of God. (no. 68)

What was the original condition of the human person according to the plan of God?

In creating man and woman God had given them a special participation in his own divine life in holiness and justice. In the plan of God they would not have had to suffer or die. Furthermore, a perfect harmony held sway within the human person, a harmony between creature and Creator, between man and woman, as well as between the first human couple and all of creation. (no. 72)

PASTORAL TEACHINGS OF THE CATHOLIC BISHOPS OF THE UNITED STATES

﹥⚶ *Economic Justice for All* ⚶﹤

THE BLESSINGS OF CREATION

Sharing the Responsibility for the Earth and Its Blessings

All people on this globe share a common ecological environment that is under increasing pressure. Depletion of soil, water, and other natural resources endangers the future. Pollution of air and water threatens the delicate balance of the biosphere on which future generations will depend.[7] The resources of the earth have been created by God for the benefit of all, and we who are alive today hold them in trust. This is a challenge to develop a new ecological ethic which will help shape a future that is both just and sustainable. (no. 12)

---

7   Synod of Bishops, *Justice in the World* (1971), 8; Pope John Paul II, *Redeemer of Man* (1979), 15.

Creation Is a Gift That We Are to Steward

At the summit of creation stands the creation of man and woman, made in God's image (Gn 1:26-27). *As such every human being possesses an inalienable dignity that stamps human existence prior to any division into races or nations and prior to human labor and human achievement* (Gn 4-11). Men and women are also to share in the creative activity of God. They are to be fruitful, to care for the earth (Gn 2:15), and to have "dominion" over it (Gn 1:28), which means they are "to govern the world in holiness and justice, and to

75

render judgment in integrity of heart" (Wis 9:3). Creation is a gift; women and men are to be faithful stewards in caring for the earth. They can justly consider that by their labor they are unfolding the Creator's work.[3] (no. 32)

3   C. Westermann, Creation (Philadelphia: Fortress Press, 1974); and B. Vawter, On Genesis: A New Reading (Garden City, N.Y.: Doubleday, 1977). See also Pastoral Constitution, no. 34.

Creation a Gift to All Men and Women

Every human person is created as an image of God, and the denial of dignity to a person is a blot on this image. Creation is a gift to all men and women, not to be appropriated for the benefit of a few; its beauty is an object of joy and reverence. The same God who came to the aid of an oppressed people and formed them into a covenant community continues to hear the cries of the oppressed and to create communities which are responsive to God's word. God's love and life are present when people can live in a community of faith and hope. (no. 40)

HONORING THE CREATOR

Reverence of God

The narratives of Genesis 1-11 also portray the origin of the strife and suffering that mar the world. Though created to enjoy intimacy with God and the fruits of the earth, Adam and Eve disrupted God's design by trying to live independently of God through a denial of their status as creatures. They turned away from God and gave to God's creation the obedience due to God alone. For this reason the prime sin in so much of the biblical tradition is idolatry: service of the creature rather than of the creator (Rom 1:25), and the attempt to overturn creation by making God in human likeness. (no. 33)

Sin and Restoration of Relationship with God

The Bible castigates not only the worship of idols, but also manifestations of idolatry, such as the quest for unrestrained power and the desire for great wealth (Is 40:12-20; 44:1-20; Wis 13:1-14:31; Col 3:5, "the greed that is idolatry"). The sin of our first parents had other consequences as well. Alienation from God pits brother against brother (Gn 4:8-16) in a cycle of war and vengeance (Gn 4:22-23). Sin and evil abound, and the primeval history culminates with another assault on the heavens, this time ending in a babble of tongues scattered over the face of the earth (Gn 11:1-9). Sin simultaneously alienates human beings from God and shatters the solidarity of the human community. Yet this reign of sin is not the final word. The primeval history is followed by the call of Abraham, a man of faith, who was to be the bearer of the promise to many nations (Gn 12:1-4). Throughout the Bible we find this struggle between sin and repentance. God's judgment on evil is followed by God's seeking out a sinful people. (no. 33)

Honoring the Creator and God's Creation

The biblical vision of creation has provided one of the most enduring legacies of church teaching. To stand before God as the Creator is to respect God's creation, both the world of nature and of human history. *From the patristic period to the present, the Church has affirmed that misuse of the world's resources or appropriation of them by a minority of the world's population betrays the gift of creation since "whatever belongs to God belongs to all."*[4] (no. 34)

---

4   St. Cyprian, *On Works and Almsgiving*, 25, trans. R. J. Deferrari, *St. Cyprian: Treatises*, 36 (New York: Fathers of the Church, 1958), 251. Original text in Migne, Patrologia

Latina, vol. 4, 620. *On the Patristic teaching*, see C. Avila, *Ownership: Early Christian Teaching* (Maryknoll, N.Y.: Orbis Books, 1983). Collection of original texts and translations.

Food, Water, Energy: Foundations of God's Gift of Life

The fundamental test of an economy is its ability to meet the essential human needs of this generation and future generations in an equitable fashion. Food, water, and energy are essential to life; their abundance in the United States has tended to make us complacent. But these goods—the foundation of God's gift of life—are too crucial to be taken for granted. God reminded the people of Israel that "the land is mine; for you are strangers and guests with me" (Lv 25:23, RSV). (no. 216)

Collaborating with the Creator

Our Christian faith calls us to contemplate God's creative and sustaining action and to measure our own collaboration with the Creator in using the earth's resources to meet human needs. While Catholic social teaching on the care of the environment and the management of natural resources is still in the process of development, a Christian moral perspective clearly gives weight and urgency to their use in meeting human needs. (no. 216)

▷▷▷ *To Be a Christian Steward: A Summary* ◁◁◁

Stewards of Creation

The Bible contains a profound message about the stewardship of material creation: God created the world, but entrusts it to human beings. Caring for and cultivating the world involves the following:

- Joyful appreciation for the God-given beauty and wonder of nature;

- Protection and preservation of the environment, which is the stewardship of ecological concern;
- Respect for human life—shielding life from threat and assault and doing everything that can be done to enhance this gift and make life flourish;
- Development of this world through noble human effort—physical labor, the trades and professions, the arts and sciences.

A Divine-Human Collaboration in Creation

Work is a fulfilling human vocation. The Second Vatican Council points out that, through work, we build up not only our world but also the Kingdom of God, already present among us. Work is a partnership with God—our share in a divine human collaboration in creation. It occupies a central place in our lives as Christian stewards.

⟩⟩ *Renewing the Earth* ⟨⟨

MORAL ROOTS AND ENVIRONMENTAL CONCERNS

A Moral Challenge

The environmental crisis is a moral challenge. It calls us to examine how we use and share the goods of the earth, what we pass on to future generations, and how we live in harmony with God's creation. (Sect. I)

The Scope of Environmental Symptoms

The effects of environmental degradation surround us: the smog in our cities; chemicals in our water and on our food; eroded topsoil blowing in the wind; the loss of valuable wetlands; radioactive and toxic waste lacking adequate disposal sites; threats to the health of industrial and farm workers. . . .

Opinions vary about the causes and the seriousness of environmental problems. Still, we can experience their effects in polluted air and water; in oil and wastes on our beaches; in the loss of farmland, wetlands, and forests; and in the decline of rivers and lakes. Scientists identify several other less visible but particularly urgent problems currently being debated by the scientific community, including depletion of the ozone layer, deforestation, the extinction of species, the generation and disposal of toxic and nuclear waste, and global warming. (Sect. I)

Human Injustice Causes Suffering in Nature

In the Bible's account of Noah, the world's new beginning was marked by the estrangement of humans from nature. The sins of humankind laid waste the land. Hosea, for example, cries out:

There is no fidelity, no mercy,
  no knowledge of God in the land.

False swearing, lying, murder, stealing and adultery!
  in their lawlessness, bloodshed follows bloodshed.

Therefore, the land mourns,
  and everything that dwells in it languishes:

The beasts of the field,
  the birds of the air,
  and even the fish of the sea perish

(Hos 4:1b-3, NAB).

In the biblical vision, therefore, injustice results in suffering for all creation. (Sect. II.A)

War Damages Creation

War represents a serious threat to the environment . . . The pursuit of peace–lasting peace based on justice–ought to be an environmental priority because the earth itself bears the wounds and scars of war. (Sect. III.I)

HOW TO PROTECT CREATION

Protect Human Life and Dignity

The web of life is one. Our mistreatment of the natural world diminishes our own dignity and sacredness, not only because we are destroying resources that future generations of humans need, but because we are engaging in actions that contradict what it means to be human. Our tradition calls us to protect the life and dignity of the human person, and it is increasingly clear that this task cannot be separated from the care and defense of all of creation. (Sect. I.A)

Preserve Nature and Make It Fruitful

Safeguarding creation requires us to live responsibly within it, rather than manage creation as though we are outside it. The human family is charged with preserving the beauty, diversity, and integrity of nature, as well as with fostering its productivity. (Sect. II.A)

CREATOR GOD, PRESENT IN CREATION

God's Presence in the Universe

The whole universe is God's dwelling. . . . The first man and woman walked with God in the cool of the day. Throughout history, people have continued to meet the Creator on mountaintops, in vast deserts, and alongside waterfalls and gently flowing springs. In storms and earthquakes, they found expressions of divine power. In the cycle of the seasons and the courses of the stars, they have discerned signs of God's fidelity and wisdom. We still share . . . in that sense of God's presence in nature. (Sect. III.A)

Creation Reveals God's Glory

The diversity of life manifests God's glory. Every creature shares a bit of the divine beauty. Because the divine goodness could not be represented by one creature alone, Aquinas tells us, God "produced many and diverse creatures, so that what was wanting to one in representation of the divine goodness might be supplied by another . . . hence the whole universe together participates in the divine goodness more perfectly, and represents it better than any single creature whatever" (*Summa Theologica*, *Prima Pars*, question 48, ad 2). (Sect. III.B)

A CHRISTIAN VISION FOR THE FUTURE OF CREATION

Responsible for Nature's Thriving

Humanity stands responsible for ensuring that all nature can continue to thrive as God intended. . . . We are not free, therefore, to use created things capriciously. (Sect. II.A)

Rest for All Creation

To curb the abuse of the land and of fellow humans, ancient Israel set out legal protections aimed at restoring the original balance between land and people (see Lv 25). Every seventh year, the land and people were to rest; nature would be restored by human restraint. And every seventh day, the Sabbath rest gave relief from unremitting toil to workers and beasts alike. It invited the whole community to taste the goodness of God in creation. In worship, moreover, the Sabbath continues to remind us of our dependence on God as his creatures, and so of our kinship with all that God has made. (Sect. II.A)

Restoration of Between Humanity and Nature in Christ

The new covenant made in Jesus' blood overcomes all hostility and restores the order of love. Just as in his person Christ has destroyed the hostility that divided people from one another, so he has overcome the opposition between humanity and nature. For he is the firstborn of a new creation and gives his Spirit to renew the whole earth (see Col 2:18; Ps 104:30). (Sect. II.B)

Creatures Are God's Creatures, with Independent Value

It is appropriate that we treat other creatures and the natural world not just as means to human fulfillment but also as God's creatures, possessing an independent value, worthy of our respect and care. (Sect. III.B)

Created Things Belong to the Entire Human Family

We are obligated to work for a just economic system which equitably shares the bounty of the earth and of human enterprise with all peoples. Created things belong not to the few, but to the entire human family. (Sect. III.E)

Care for Vulnerable Creatures

We are charged with restoring the integrity of all creation. We must care for all God's creatures, especially the most vulnerable. (Sect. III.H)

An Ordered Love for Creation

An ordered love for creation, therefore, is ecological without being ecocentric. We can and must care for the earth without mistaking it for the ultimate object of our devotion. A Christian love of the natural world, as St. Francis showed us, can restrain grasping and wanton human behavior and help mightily to preserve and nurture all that God has made. (Sect. IV.A)

The Future of the Earth

Guided by the Spirit of God, the future of the earth lies in human hands. . . . Even as humanity's mistakes are at the root of earth's travail today, human talents and invention can and must assist in its rebirth and contribute to human development. (Sect. IV.B)

Applying Indigenous and Scientific Technologies

Reverence for nature must be combined with scientific learning. . . . The ecological crisis heightens our awareness of the need for new approaches to scientific research and technology. Many indigenous technologies can teach us much. Such technologies are more compatible with the ecosystem, are more available to poor persons, and are more sustainable for the entire community. (Sect. IV.B)

Christian Love

Christian love forbids choosing between people and the planet. It urges us to work for an equitable and sustainable future in which all peoples can share in the bounty of the earth and in which the earth itself is protected. (Sect. IV.C)

Humanity Has A Decision to Make

Today, humanity is at a crossroads. Having read the signs of the times, we can either ignore the harm we see and witness further damage, or we can take up our responsibilities to the Creator and creation with renewed courage and commitment. (Sect. V)

Called to Conversion

The environmental crisis of our own day constitutes an exceptional call to conversion. As individuals, as institutions, as a people, we need a change of heart to save the planet for our children and generations yet unborn. (Sect. V.C)

✥ Global Climate Change ✥

THE CLIMATE DILEMMA

Scientific Consensus of the Human Impact

Responsible scientific research is always careful to recognize uncertainty and is modest in its claims. Yet over the past few decades, the evidence of global climate change and the emerging scientific consensus about the human impact on this process have led many governments to reach the conclusion that they need to invest time, money, and political will to address the problem through collective international action. (p. 5)

Environmental Impacts May Have Broad Reach

The earth's atmosphere encompasses all people, creatures, and habitats. The melting of ice sheets and glaciers, the destruction of rain forests, and the pollution of water in one place can have environmental impacts elsewhere. As Pope John Paul II has said, "We cannot interfere in one area of the ecosystem without paying due attention both to the consequences of such interference in other areas and to the well being of future generations" (Dec. 8, 1989). Responses to global climate change should reflect our interdependence and common responsibility for the future of our planet. (pp. 7-8)

Responsibility Toward Future Generations

Passing along the problem of global climate change to future generations as a result of our delay, indecision, or self-interest would be easy. But we simply cannot leave this problem for the children of tomorrow. As stewards of their heritage, we have an obligation to respect their dignity and to pass on their natural inheritance, so that their lives are protected and, if possible, made better than our own. (p. 9)

Obligations to Assist the Resource-Poor

The common good requires solidarity with the poor who are often without the resources to face many problems, including the potential impacts of climate change. Our obligations to the one human family stretch across space and time. They tie us to the poor in our midst and across the globe, as well as to future generations. The commandment to love our neighbor invites us to consider the poor and marginalized of other nations as true brothers and sisters who share with us the one table of life intended by God for the enjoyment of all. (pp. 10-11)

Protect the Atmosphere that Supports Life

The atmosphere that supports life on earth is a God-given gift, one we must respect and protect. It unites us as one human family. If we harm the atmosphere, we dishonor our Creator and the gift of creation. The values of our faith call us to humility, sacrifice, and a respect for life and the natural gifts God has provided. (p. 17)

TOOLS AND SOLUTIONS

Prudence Applies Intelligence to Actions

The virtue of prudence is paramount in addressing climate change. . . . Prudence is intelligence applied to our actions. It allows us to discern what constitutes the common good in a given situation. Prudence requires a deliberate and reflective process that aids in the shaping of the community's conscience. Prudence not only helps us identify the principles at stake in a given issue, but also moves us to adopt courses of action to protect the common good. Prudence is not, as popularly thought, simply a cautious and safe approach to decisions. Rather, it is a thoughtful, deliberate, and reasoned basis for taking or avoiding action to achieve a moral good. (p. 6)

Human Ingenuity Will Help Solve the Crisis

Economic freedom, initiative, and creativity are essential to help our nation find effective ways to address climate change. The

United States' history of economic, technological innovation, and entrepreneurship invites us to move beyond status quo responses to this challenge. In addition, the right to private property is matched by the responsibility to use what we own to serve the common good. (p. 8)

Pursue Better Energy Use, Change Lifestyle

Technological innovation and entrepreneurship can help make possible options that can lead us to a more environmentally benign energy path. Changes in lifestyle based on traditional moral virtues can ease the way to a sustainable and equitable world economy in which sacrifice will no longer be an unpopular concept. For many of us, a life less focused on material gain may remind us that we are more than what we have. Rejecting the false promises of excessive or conspicuous consumption can even allow more time for family, friends, and civic responsibilities. A renewed sense of sacrifice and restraint could make an essential contribution to addressing global climate change. (p. 9)

Share Energy-Friendly Know-How

Wealthier industrialized nations have the resources, know-how, and entrepreneurship to produce more efficient cars and cleaner industries. These countries need to share these emerging technologies with the less-developed countries and assume more of the financial responsibility that would enable poorer countries to afford them. (p. 11)

Sacred Scripture

OLD TESTAMENT

✺ The Pentateuch ✺

GENESIS

The Story of Creation
(Genesis Chapter 1)

In the beginning, when God created the heavens and the earth—
and the earth was without form or shape, with darkness over the
abyss and a mighty wind sweeping over the waters—Then God said:
Let there be light, and there was light. God saw that the light was
good. God then separated the light from the darkness. God called
the light "day," and the darkness he called "night."

Evening came, and morning followed—the first day.

Then God said: Let there be a dome in the middle of the waters,
to separate one body of water from the other. God made the dome,
and it separated the water below the dome from the water above the
dome. And so it happened. God called the dome "sky."

Evening came, and morning followed—the second day.

Then God said: Let the water under the sky be gathered into a
single basin, so that the dry land may appear. And so it happened:
the water under the sky was gathered into its basin, and the dry land
appeared. God called the dry land "earth," and the basin of water he
called "sea." God saw that it was good.

Then God said: Let the earth bring forth vegetation: every
kind of plant that bears seed and every kind of fruit tree on earth
that bears fruit with its seed in it. And so it happened: the earth
brought forth vegetation: every kind of plant that bears seed and
every kind of fruit tree that bears fruit with its seed in it. God saw
that it was good.

Evening came, and morning followed—the third day.

Then God said: Let there be lights in the dome of the sky, to separate day from night. Let them mark the seasons, the days and the years, and serve as lights in the dome of the sky, to illuminate the earth. And so it happened: God made the two great lights, the greater one to govern the day, and the lesser one to govern the night, and the stars. God set them in the dome of the sky, to illuminate the earth, to govern the day and the night, and to separate the light from the darkness. God saw that it was good.

Evening came, and morning followed—the fourth day.

Then God said: Let the water teem with an abundance of living creatures, and on the earth let birds fly beneath the dome of the sky. God created the great sea monsters and all kinds of crawling living creatures with which the water teems, and all kinds of winged birds. God saw that it was good, and God blessed them, saying: Be fertile, multiply, and fill the water of the seas; and let the birds multiply on the earth.

Evening came, and morning followed—the fifth day.

Then God said: Let the earth bring forth every kind of living creature: tame animals, crawling things, and every kind of wild animal. And so it happened: God made every kind of wild animal, every kind of tame animal, and every kind of thing that crawls on the ground. God saw that it was good.

Then God said: Let us make human beings in our image, after our likeness. Let them have dominion over the fish of the sea, the birds of the air, the tame animals, all the wild animals, and all the creatures that crawl on the earth.

God created mankind in his image;

in the image of God he created them;

male and female he created them.

God blessed them and God said to them: Be fertile and multiply; fill the earth and subdue it. Have dominion over the fish of the sea, the birds of the air, and all the living things that crawl on the earth.

God also said: See, I give you every seed-bearing plant on all the earth and every tree that has seed-bearing fruit on it to be your food; and to all the wild animals, all the birds of the air, and all the living creatures that crawl on the earth, I give all the green plants for food. And so it happened.

God looked at everything he had made, and found it very good. Evening came, and morning followed—the sixth day.

DEUTERONOMY

The Heavens and the Earth Belong to the Lord
(Deuteronomy 10:14)

The heavens, even the highest heavens, belong to the LORD, your God, as well as the earth and everything on it.

⟩⟩⟩ The History Books ⟨⟨⟨

NEHEMIAH

Creator God
(Nehemiah 9:5-6)

"Arise, bless the LORD, your God, from eternity to eternity!"

"And may they bless your glorious name,
    which is exalted above all blessing and praise."

"You are the LORD, you alone;

You made the heavens,
    the highest heavens and all their host,

The earth and all that is upon it,
    the seas and all that is in them.

To all of them you give life,
    the heavenly hosts bow down before you.

JUDITH

Let Every Creature Serve God
(Judith 16:13-15)

"I will sing a new song to my God.
    O Lord, great are you and glorious,
        marvelous in power and unsurpassable.

Let your every creature serve you;
    for you spoke, and they were made.

You sent forth your spirit, and it created them;
    no one can resist your voice.

For the mountains to their bases
    are tossed with the waters;
        the rocks, like wax, melt before your glance.

"But to those who fear you,
    you will show mercy."

›✳̇✠ The Wisdom Books ✠̇✳‹

PSALMS

Stewards over the Works of God's Hand
(Psalm 8:2-10)

O LORD, our Lord,
  how awesome is your name through all the earth!

I will sing of your majesty above the heavens
  with the mouths of babes and infants.

You have established a bulwark against your foes,
  to silence enemy and avenger.

When I see your heavens, the work of your fingers,
  the moon and stars that you set in place—

What is man that you are mindful of him,
  and a son of man that you care for him?

Yet you have made him little less than a god,
  crowned him with glory and honor.

You have given him rule over the works of your hands,
  put all things at his feet:

All sheep and oxen,
  even the beasts of the field,

The birds of the air, the fish of the sea,
  and whatever swims the paths of the seas.

O LORD, our Lord,
    how awesome is your name through all the earth!

Creation Reveals the Glory of God
(Psalm 19:2-7)

The heavens declare the glory of God;
    the firmament proclaims the works of his hands.

Day unto day pours forth speech;
    night unto night whispers knowledge.

There is no speech, no words;
    their voice is not heard;

A report goes forth through all the earth,
    their messages, to the ends of the world.

He has pitched in them a tent for the sun;
    it comes forth like a bridegroom from his canopy,
    and like a hero joyfully runs its course.

From one end of the heavens it comes forth;
    its course runs through to the other;
    nothing escapes its heat.

The Earth Is the Lord's
(Psalm 24:1)

The earth is the LORD's and all it holds,
    the world and those who dwell in it.

Divine Gardener of the Earth
(Psalm 65:2, 6-14)

To you we owe our hymn of praise,
    O God on Zion.

You answer us with awesome deeds of justice,
    O God our savior,

The hope of all the ends of the earth
    and of those far off across the sea.

You are robed in power,
    you set up the mountains by your might.

You still the roaring of the seas,
    the roaring of their waves,
    the tumult of the peoples.

Distant peoples stand in awe of your marvels;
    the places of morning and evening you make resound with joy.

You visit the earth and water it,
    make it abundantly fertile.

God's stream is filled with water;
    you supply their grain.

Thus do you prepare it:
    you drench its plowed furrows,
    and level its ridges.

With showers you keep it soft,
    blessing its young sprouts.

You adorn the year with your bounty;
　　your paths drip with fruitful rain.

The meadows of the wilderness also drip;
　　the hills are robed with joy.

The pastures are clothed with flocks,
　　the valleys blanketed with grain;
　　they cheer and sing for joy.

Hymn to God the Creator
(Psalm 104)

Bless the LORD, my soul!
　　LORD, my God, you are great indeed!

You are clothed with majesty and splendor,
　　robed in light as with a cloak.

You spread out the heavens like a tent;
　　setting the beams of your chambers upon the waters.

You make the clouds your chariot;
　　traveling on the wings of the wind.

You make the winds your messengers;
　　flaming fire, your ministers.

You fixed the earth on its foundation,
　　so it can never be shaken.

The deeps covered it like a garment;
　　above the mountains stood the waters.

At your rebuke they took flight;
　　at the sound of your thunder they fled.

They rushed up the mountains, down the valleys
    to the place you had fixed for them.

You set a limit they cannot pass;
    never again will they cover the earth.

You made springs flow in wadies
    that wind among the mountains.

They give drink to every beast of the field;
    here wild asses quench their thirst.

Beside them the birds of heaven nest;
    among the branches they sing.

You water the mountains from your chambers;
    from the fruit of your labor the earth abounds.

You make the grass grow for the cattle
    and plants for people's work
    to bring forth food from the earth,

wine to gladden their hearts,
    oil to make their faces shine,
    and bread to sustain the human heart.

The trees of the Lord drink their fill,
    the cedars of Lebanon, which you planted.

There the birds build their nests;
    the stork in the junipers, its home.

The high mountains are for wild goats;
    the rocky cliffs, a refuge for badgers.

You made the moon to mark the seasons,
    the sun that knows the hour of its setting.

You bring darkness and night falls,
 then all the animals of the forest wander about.

Young lions roar for prey;
 they seek their food from God.

When the sun rises, they steal away
 and settle down in their dens.

People go out to their work,
 to their labor till evening falls.

How varied are your works, LORD!
 In wisdom you have made them all;
 the earth is full of your creatures.

There is the sea, great and wide!
 It teems with countless beings,
 living things both large and small.

There ships ply their course
 and Leviathan, whom you formed to play with.

All of these look to you
 to give them food in due time.

When you give it to them, they gather;
 when you open your hand, they are well filled.

When you hide your face, they panic.
 Take away their breath, they perish
 and return to the dust.

Send forth your spirit, they are created
 and you renew the face of the earth.

May the glory of the LORD endure forever;
  may the LORD be glad in his works!

Who looks at the earth and it trembles,
  touches the mountains and they smoke!

I will sing to the LORD all my life;
  I will sing praise to my God while I live.

May my meditation be pleasing to him;
  I will rejoice in the LORD.

May sinners vanish from the earth,
  and the wicked be no more.

Bless the LORD, my soul! Hallelujah!

All You Creatures, Praise the Lord (Psalm 148)

Hallelujah!

Praise the LORD from the heavens;
  praise him in the heights.

Praise him, all you his angels;
  give praise, all you his hosts.

Praise him, sun and moon;
  praise him, all shining stars.

Praise him, highest heavens,
  you waters above the heavens.

Let them all praise the LORD's name;
  for he commanded and they were created,

Assigned them their station forever,
    set an order that will never change.

Praise the LORD from the earth,
    you sea monsters and all the deeps of the sea;

Lightning and hail, snow and thick clouds,
    storm wind that fulfills his command;

Mountains and all hills,
    fruit trees and all cedars;

Animals wild and tame,
    creatures that crawl and birds that fly;

Kings of the earth and all peoples,
    princes and all who govern on earth;

Young men and women too,
    old and young alike.

Let them all praise the LORD's name,
    for his name alone is exalted,

His majesty above earth and heaven.

He has lifted high the horn of his people;
    to the praise of all his faithful,
    the Israelites, the people near to him.

Hallelujah!

Wisdom

God's Spirit Fills the Earth
(Wisdom 1:7)

For the spirit of the LORD fills the world,
    is all-embracing, and knows whatever is said.

Prayer for Wisdom to Govern the World in Holiness and Righteousness
(Wisdom 9:1-6, 9-12, 17-18)

God of my ancestors, Lord of mercy,
    you who have made all things by your word

And in your wisdom have established humankind
    to rule the creatures produced by you,

And to govern the world in holiness and righteousness,
    and to render judgment in integrity of heart

Give me Wisdom, the consort at your throne,
    and do not reject me from among your children;

For I am your servant, the child of your maidservant,
    a man weak and short-lived
    and lacking in comprehension of judgment and of laws.

Indeed, though one be perfect among mortals,
    if Wisdom, who comes from you, be lacking,
    that one will count for nothing.

Now with you is Wisdom, who knows your works
  and was present when you made the world;

Who understands what is pleasing in your eyes
  and what is conformable with your commands.

Send her forth from your holy heavens
  and from your glorious throne dispatch her

That she may be with me and work with me,
  that I may know what is pleasing to you.

For she knows and understands all things,
  and will guide me prudently in my affairs
  and safeguard me by her glory;

Thus my deeds will be acceptable,
  and I will judge your people justly
  and be worthy of my father's throne.

✣

Or who can know your counsel, unless you give Wisdom
  and send your holy spirit from on high?

Thus were the paths of those on earth made straight,
  and people learned what pleases you,
  and were saved by Wisdom.

"You Love All Things That Are"
(Wisdom 11:22-26, 12:1)

Indeed, before you the whole universe is like a grain from
        a balance,
  or a drop of morning dew come down upon the earth.

But you have mercy on all, because you can do all things;
    and you overlook sins for the sake of repentance.

For you love all things that are
    and loathe nothing that you have made;
    for you would not fashion what you hate.

How could a thing remain, unless you willed it;
    or be preserved, had it not been called forth by you?

But you spare all things, because they are yours,
    O Ruler and Lover of souls,
    for your imperishable spirit is in all things!

SIRACH

"Divine Wisdom Seen in Creation"
(Sirach 16:24-30)

Listen to me, my son, and take my advice,
    and apply your mind to my words,

While I pour out my spirit by measure
    and impart knowledge with care.

When at the first God created his works
    and, as he made them, assigned their tasks,

He arranged for all time what they were to do,
    their domains from generation to generation.

They were not to go hungry or grow weary,
    or ever cease from their tasks.

Never does a single one crowd its neighbor,
    or do any ever disobey his word.

Then the Lord looked upon the earth,
    and filled it with his blessings.

Its surface he covered with every kind of living creature
    which must return into it again.

Declare God's Mighty Works in Creation (Sirach 42:15-25)

Now will I recall God's works;
    what I have seen, I will describe.

By the LORD's word his works were brought into being;
    he accepts the one who does his will.

As the shining sun is clear to all,
    so the glory of the LORD fills all his works;

Yet even God's holy ones must fail
    in recounting the wonders of the LORD,

Though God has given his hosts the strength
    to stand firm before his glory.

He searches out the abyss and penetrates the heart;
    their secrets he understands.

For the Most High possesses all knowledge,
    and sees from of old the things that are to come.

He makes known the past and the future,
    and reveals the deepest secrets.

He lacks no understanding;
    no single thing escapes him.

He regulates the mighty deeds of his wisdom;
    he is from all eternity one and the same,

With nothing added, nothing taken away;
    no need of a counselor for him!

How beautiful are all his works,
    delightful to gaze upon and a joy to behold!

Everything lives and abides forever;
    and to meet each need all things are preserved.

All of them differ, one from another,
    yet none of them has he made in vain;

For each in turn, as it comes, is good;
    can one ever see enough of their splendor?

>⯈ The Prophetic Books ⯇

ISAIAH

**Creation Sings Praises to God for Humanity's Redemption
(Isaiah 44:23)**

Raise a glad cry, you heavens—the LORD has acted!
    Shout, you depths of the earth.

Break forth, mountains, into song,
    forest, with all your trees.

For the LORD has redeemed Jacob,
    shows his glory through Israel.

DANIEL

All Creation, Bless the Lord
(Daniel 3:51-90)

Then these three in the furnace with one voice sang, glorifying and blessing God:

"Blessed are you, O Lord, the God of our ancestors,
    praiseworthy and exalted above all forever;

And blessed is your holy and glorious name,
    praiseworthy and exalted above all for all ages.

Blessed are you in the temple of your holy glory,
    praiseworthy and glorious above all forever.

Blessed are you on the throne of your kingdom,
    praiseworthy and exalted above all forever.

Blessed are you who look into the depths
    from your throne upon the cherubim,
    praiseworthy and exalted above all forever.

Blessed are you in the firmament of heaven,
    praiseworthy and glorious forever.

Bless the Lord, all you works of the Lord,
    praise and exalt him above all forever.

Angels of the Lord, bless the Lord,
    praise and exalt him above all forever.

You heavens, bless the Lord,
    praise and exalt him above all forever.

All you waters above the heavens, bless the Lord,
    praise and exalt him above all forever.

All you powers, bless the Lord;
    praise and exalt him above all forever.

Sun and moon, bless the Lord;
    praise and exalt him above all forever.

Stars of heaven, bless the Lord;
    praise and exalt him above all forever.

Every shower and dew, bless the Lord;
    praise and exalt him above all forever.

All you winds, bless the Lord;
    praise and exalt him above all forever.

Fire and heat, bless the Lord;
    praise and exalt him above all forever.

Cold and chill, bless the Lord;
    praise and exalt him above all forever.

Dew and rain, bless the Lord;
    praise and exalt him above all forever.

Frost and chill, bless the Lord;
    praise and exalt him above all forever.

Hoarfrost and snow, bless the Lord;
    praise and exalt him above all forever.

Nights and days, bless the Lord;
    praise and exalt him above all forever.

Light and darkness, bless the Lord;
    praise and exalt him above all forever.

Lightnings and clouds, bless the Lord;
    praise and exalt him above all forever.

Let the earth bless the Lord,
    praise and exalt him above all forever.

Mountains and hills, bless the Lord;
    praise and exalt him above all forever.

Everything growing on earth, bless the Lord;
    praise and exalt him above all forever.

You springs, bless the Lord;
    praise and exalt him above all forever.

Seas and rivers, bless the Lord;
    praise and exalt him above all forever.

You sea monsters and all water creatures, bless the Lord;
    praise and exalt him above all forever.

All you birds of the air, bless the Lord;
    praise and exalt him above all forever.

All you beasts, wild and tame, bless the Lord;
    praise and exalt him above all forever.

All you mortals, bless the Lord;
    praise and exalt him above all forever.

O Israel, bless the Lord;
    praise and exalt him above all forever.

Priests of the Lord, bless the Lord;
    praise and exalt him above all forever.

Servants of the Lord, bless the Lord;
  praise and exalt him above all forever.

Spirits and souls of the just, bless the Lord;
  praise and exalt him above all forever.

Holy and humble of heart, bless the Lord;
  praise and exalt him above all forever.

Hananiah, Azariah, Mishael, bless the Lord;
  praise and exalt him above all forever.

For he has delivered us from Sheol,
  and saved us from the power of death;

He has freed us from the raging flame
  and delivered us from the fire.

Give thanks to the Lord, who is good,
  whose mercy endures forever.

Bless the God of gods, all you who fear the Lord;
  praise and give thanks,
  for his mercy endures forever."

HOSEA

God's Covenant with Creatures
(Hosea 2:20-22)

I will make a covenant for them on that day,
  with the wild animals,

With the birds of the air,
  and with the things that crawl on the ground.

Bow and sword and warfare
    I will destroy from the land,
    and I will give them rest in safety.

I will betroth you to me forever:
    I will betroth you to me with justice and with judgment,
    with loyalty and with compassion;

I will betroth you to me with fidelity,
    and you shall know the LORD.

NEW TESTAMENT

﹩ The Gospels and Acts ﹩

MARK

Proclaim the Gospel to All Creation
(Mark 16:15)

"He said to them, "Go into the whole world and proclaim the gospel to every creature.""

LUKE

More Expected of To Whom More Is Given
(Luke 12:48)

Much will be required of the person entrusted with much, and still more will be demanded of the person entrusted with more.

Creation Praises God
(Luke 19:35-40)

They brought [the colt] to Jesus, threw their cloaks over the colt, and helped Jesus to mount. As he rode along, the people were spreading their cloaks on the road; and now as he was approaching the slope of the Mount of Olives, the whole multitude of his disciples began to praise God aloud with joy for all the mighty deeds they had seen. They proclaimed:

"Blessed is the king who comes
    in the name of the Lord.

Peace in heaven
  and glory in the highest."

Some of the Pharisees in the crowd said to him, "Teacher, rebuke your disciples." He said in reply, "I tell you, if they keep silent, the stones will cry out!"

JOHN

In the Beginning . . . A New Creation Story
(John 1:1-5)

In the beginning was the Word, and the Word was with God, and the Word was God. He was in the beginning with God. All things came to be through him, and without him nothing came to be. What came to be through him was life, and this life was the light of the human race; the light shines in the darkness, and the darkness has not overcome it.

Multiplication of Loaves: Don't Waste What the Lord Provides
(John 6:5-13)

When Jesus raised his eyes and saw that a large crowd was coming to him, he said to Philip, "Where can we buy enough food for them to eat?" He said this to test him, because he himself knew what he was going to do. Philip answered him, "Two hundred days' wages worth of food would not be enough for each of them to have a little [bit]." One of his disciples, Andrew, the brother of Simon Peter, said to him, "There is a boy here who has five barley loaves and two fish; but what good are these for so many?" Jesus said, "Have the people recline." Now there was a great deal of grass in that place. So the men reclined, about five thousand in number. Then Jesus took the loaves, gave thanks, and distributed them to those who were reclining, and also as much of the fish as they wanted. When they had had their fill, he said to his disciples, "Gather the fragments left over, so that nothing will be wasted." So they collected them, and filled twelve wicker baskets with fragments from the five barley loaves that had been more than they could eat.

Acts

God, the Giver of Life, Established the Laws of Nature (17:24-28)

The God who made the world and all that is in it, the Lord of heaven and earth . . . it is he who gives to everyone life and breath and everything. He made from one the whole human race to dwell on the entire surface of the earth, and he fixed the ordered seasons and the boundaries of their regions, so that people might seek God, even perhaps grope for him and find him, though indeed he is not far from any one of us. For 'In him we live and move and have our being,' as even some of your poets have said, 'For we too are his offspring.'

❧ The New Testament Letters ❧

Romans

God's Power and Divinity Evident in Creation
(Romans 1:19-20)

What can be known about God is evident to them, because God made it evident to them. Ever since the creation of the world, his invisible attributes of eternal power and divinity have been able to be understood and perceived in what he has made.

Creation Awaits the Revelation of the Children of God
(Romans 8:19-21)

Creation awaits with eager expectation the revelation of the children of God; for creation was made subject to futility, not of its own accord but because of the one who subjected it, in hope that creation itself would be set free from slavery to corruption and share in the glorious freedom of the children of God.

1 Corinthians

All Things "Are" from the Father and Through the Son
(1 Corinthians 8:6)

Yet for us there is
one God, the Father,
   from whom all things are and for whom we exist,

and one Lord, Jesus Christ,
  through whom all things are and through whom we exist.

---

2 CORINTHIANS

A New Creation
(2 Corinthians 5:17)

Whoever is in Christ is a new creation: the old things
have passed away; behold, new things have come.

COLOSSIANS

Christ, the Firstborn of All Creation
(Colossians 1:15-20)

He is the image of the invisible God,
  the firstborn of all creation.

For in him were created all things in heaven and on earth,
  the visible and the invisible,
  whether thrones or dominions or principalities or powers;
  all things were created through him and for him.

He is before all things,
  and in him all things hold together.

He is the head of the body, the church.
  He is the beginning, the firstborn from the dead,
  that in all things he himself might be preeminent.

For in him all the fullness was pleased to dwell,

and through him to reconcile all things for him,
    making peace by the blood of his cross
    [through him], whether those on earth or those in heaven.

---

1 TIMOTHY

All God Created Is Good
(1 Timothy 4:4-5)

For everything created by God is good, and nothing is to be rejected when received with thanksgiving, for it is made holy by the invocation of God in prayer.

JAMES

We Are the Firstfruits of God's Creation
(James 1:17-18)

All good giving and every perfect gift is from above, coming down from the Father of lights, with whom there is no alteration or shadow caused by change. He willed to give us birth by the word of truth that we may be a kind of firstfruits of his creatures.

Revelation

Worship in Heaven Given to God the Creator
(Revelation 4:8-11)

The four living creatures, each of them with six wings, were covered with eyes inside and out. Day and night they do not stop exclaiming:

"Holy, holy, holy is the Lord God almighty,
　who was, and who is, and who is to come."

Whenever the living creatures give glory and honor and thanks to the one who sits on the throne, who lives forever and ever, the twenty-four elders fall down before the one who sits on the throne and worship him, who lives forever and ever. They throw down their crowns before the throne, exclaiming:

"Worthy are you, Lord our God,
　to receive glory and honor and power,

for you created all things;
　because of your will they came to be and were created."

All Creation in Heaven and Earth Will Praise God
(Revelation 5:13)

Then I heard every creature in heaven and on earth and under the earth and in the sea, everything in the universe, cry out:

"To the one who sits on the throne and to the Lamb
　be blessing and honor, glory and might,
　forever and ever."

Sacred Tradition:
Prayers of the Church

PRAYERS AND BLESSINGS

Prayers of Praise

Canticle of the Sun by St. Francis of Assisi

Most high, all-powerful, good Lord,
  yours are the praises, the glory, and the honor, and all blessing,

to you alone, Most High, do they belong,
  and no human is worthy to mention your name.

Praised be you, my Lord, with all your creatures,
  especially Sir Brother Sun,
  who is the day and through whom you give us light.

And he is beautiful and radiant with great splendor;
  and bears a likeness of you, Most High One.

Praised be you, my Lord, through Sister Moon and the stars,
  in heaven you formed them clear and precious and beautiful.

Praised be you, my Lord, through Brother Wind,
  and through the air, cloudy and serene, and every kind
      of weather,
  through whom you give sustenance to your creatures.

Praised be you, my Lord, through Sister Water,
  who is very useful and humble and precious and chaste.

Praised be you, my Lord, through Brother Fire,
  through whom you light the night,
  and he is beautiful and playful and robust and strong.

Praised be you, my Lord, through our Sister Mother Earth,
    who sustains and governs us,
    and who produces various fruit with colored flowers and herbs.

Praised be you, my Lord, through those who give pardon for
        your love,
    and bear infirmity and tribulation.

Blessed are those who endure in peace
    for by you, Most High, shall they be crowned.

Praised be you, my Lord, through our Sister Bodily Death,
    from whom no one living can escape.

Woe to those who die in mortal sin.
    Blessed are those whom death will find in your most holy will,
    for the second death shall do them no harm.

Praise and bless my Lord and give him thanks
    and serve him with great humility.

PRAYERS OF INTERCESSION FOR CREATION

Prayer to the Holy Spirit

V. Come, Holy Spirit, fill the hearts of your faithful.
R. And kindle in them the fire of your love.

V. Send forth your Spirit and they shall be created.
R. And you shall renew the face of the earth.

Let us pray:

O God, by the light of the Holy Spirit you have taught the hearts of your faithful. In the same Spirit, help us to know what is truly right and always to rejoice in your consolation. We ask this through Christ, Our Lord. Amen.

Short Invocation (from the Litany of the Holy Eucharist)

Jesus, Lord of creation, have mercy on us.

Pledge of Commitment to Protect and Heal God's Creation

This Pledge of Commitment may be read in unison or in alternation:

We have come to renew our covenant with God and with one another in Christ Jesus, our Lord.

We have come to help protect God's creation.

We have come as followers of Jesus to commit ourselves anew to one another and to heal injustice and poverty.

We have come to stand together against all threats to life.

We have come to discover some new beauty every day in God's creation: the sunrise and sunset, birds, flowers and trees, rainbows in the sky, the stars, the many forms of life in the forest.

We have come to listen to the "music of the universe"—water flowing over rocks, the wind, trees bending in the wind, raindrops pattering the roof.

We will remember always that God speaks to us through the beauty of his creation, and we will try our best to answer God's call to reverence all that he has created.

Prayers of Petition

O Lord, grant us the grace to respect and care for Your creation.
Lord, hear our prayer.

O Lord, bless all of your creatures as a sign of Your wondrous love.
Lord, hear our prayer.

O Lord, help us to end the suffering of the poor and bring healing
to all of your creation.
Lord, hear our prayer.

O Lord, help us to use our technological inventiveness to undo the
damage we have done to Your creation and to sustain Your
gift of nature.
Lord, hear our prayer.

DAILY PRAYERS

PRAYERS AT MEALTIMES

Grace Before Meals

Bless us, O Lord, and these thy gifts, which we are about to receive from thy bounty, through Christ our Lord. Amen.

(*Catholic Household Blessings and Prayers*, p. 51)

Grace After Meals

We give thee thanks, for all thy benefits, almighty God, who lives and reigns forever. [*And may the souls of the faithful departed, through the mercy of God, rest in peace.*] Amen.

(*Catholic Household Blessings and Prayers*, p. 51)

⟫⟩ Prayers for Creation ⟨⟨

Prayer to Care for Our Common Home

Father of all,
Creator and ruler of the universe,
You entrusted your world to us as a gift.
Help us to care for it and all people,
that we may live in right relationship—
   with You,
   with ourselves,
   with one another,
   and with creation.

Christ our Lord,
both divine and human,

You lived among us and died for our sins.
Help us to imitate your love for the human family
by recognizing that we are all connected—
    to our brothers and sisters around the world,
    to those in poverty impacted by environmental devastation,
    and to future generations.

Holy Spirit,
giver of wisdom and love,
You breathe life in us and guide us.
Help us to live according to your vision,
stirring to action the hearts of all—
    individuals and families,
    communities of faith,
    and civil and political leaders.

Triune God, help us to hear the cry of those in poverty, and
the cry of the earth, so that we may together care for our
common home.

Amen.

(Prayer from the USCCB, based on *Laudato Si'*)

Prayers for the Blessing of Gardens, Fields, or Orchards

Let us together praise the Lord, from whom we have rain from
the heavens and abundance from the earth. Blessed be God now
and forever.

R/. Amen.

Let us bless God, whose might has created the earth and whose
providence has enriched it. God has given us the earth to cultivate,
so that we may gather its fruits to sustain life.

But as we thank God for his bounteousness, let us learn also, as the Gospel teaches, to seek first his Kingship over us, his way of holiness. Then all our needs will be given us besides.

(*Catholic Household Blessings and Prayers*, pp. 142-43)

Blessing for the Products of Nature

Blessed are you, O God,
Creator of the universe,
who have made all things good
and given the earth for us to cultivate.

Grant that we may always use created things gratefully
and share your gift with those in need,
out of the love of Christ our Lord,
who lives and reigns with you for ever and ever.

R. Amen.

(*Catholic Household Blessings and Prayers*, pp. 324-25)

PRAYERS FOR WEATHER

Prayer for Protection During a Storm

Loving God, maker of heaven and earth,
protect us in your love and mercy.

Send the Spirit of Jesus to be with us,
to still our fears and give us confidence.

In the stormy waters,
Jesus reassured his disciples by his presence,
calmed the storm, and strengthened their faith.

Guard us from harm during this storm
and renew our faith to serve you faithfully.

Give us the courage to face all difficulties
and the wisdom to see the ways
your Spirit binds us together
in mutual assistance.

With confidence we make our prayer
through Jesus Christ our Lord.

R/. Amen.

(*Catholic Household Blessings and Prayers*, pp. 334-35)

Prayer for Rain

God our Creator,
maker of all things and protector of your people,
in your love look upon us in our time of need
and give us your help.

Open the heavens for us and send us the rain
we need for our lives and crops.

As our hearts long for you,
so we seek rain to refresh the earth;
as we long for life,
so let the earth produce its harvest in abundance.

May we rejoice in the good things of the earth
and raise our eyes to you, the source of all blessings.

Hear our cry for mercy and answer our prayer,
through Jesus Christ our Lord.

R/. Amen.

(*Catholic Household Blessings and Prayers*, pp. 334-35)

Prayer for Dry Weather

Almighty God,
look with mercy on us
and swiftly come to our help.

Give us the dry weather we need,
and deliver us from (*poor crops, the danger of floods, etc.*).

Grant us the good things of the earth
and your spiritual blessings in abundance.

Teach us to be generous to others
and grateful to you for your goodness.

With confidence we make our prayer
though Jesus Christ our Lord.

R/. Amen.

(*Catholic Household Blessings and Prayers*, pp. 334-35)

PRAYERS OF THE POPES

PRAYERS OF ST. JOHN PAUL II

Evangelium Vitae Prayer

O Mary,
bright dawn of the world,
Mother of the living,
to you do we entrust the *cause of life*:

look down, O Mother, upon the vast numbers
of babies not allowed to be born,
of the poor whose lives are made difficult,
of men and women who are victims of brutal violence,
of the elderly and the sick killed by indifference
or out of misguided mercy.
Grant that all who believe in your Son
may *proclaim the Gospel of life*
with honesty and love to the people of our time.

Obtain for them the grace to *accept that Gospel*
as a gift ever new,
the joy *of celebrating* it with gratitude
throughout their lives
and the courage to *bear witness to it*
resolutely, in order to build,
together with all people of good will,
the civilization of truth and love,
to the praise and glory of God, the Creator and lover of life.

(*Catholic Household Blessings and Prayers*, p. 366)

Prayer for Peace: To Mary, the Light of Hope

Immaculate Heart of Mary,
help us to conquer the menace of evil,
which so easily takes root in the hearts of the people of today,
and whose immeasurable effects
already weigh down upon our modern world
and seem to block the paths toward the future.

From famine and war, deliver us.

From nuclear war, from incalculable self-destruction, from every kind of war, deliver us.

From sins against human life from its very beginning, deliver us.

From hatred and from the demeaning of the dignity of the children of God, deliver us.

From every kind of injustice in the life of society, both national and international, deliver us.

From readiness to trample on the commandments of God, deliver us.

From attempts to stifle in human hearts the very truth of God, deliver us.

From the loss of awareness of good and evil, deliver us.

From sins against the Holy Spirit, deliver us.

Accept, O Mother of Christ, this cry laden with the sufferings of all individual human beings, laden with the sufferings of whole societies.

Help us with the power of the Holy Spirit to conquer all sin: individual sin and the "sin of the world," sin in all its manifestations.

Let there be revealed once more in the history of the world the infinite saving power of the redemption: the power of merciful love.

May it put a stop to evil.

May it transform consciences.

May your Immaculate Heart reveal for all the light of hope.

Amen.

(*Catholic Household Blessings and Prayers*, pp. 375-76)

Prayer to Our Lady of the Divine Love

Hail, oh Mother, Queen of the world.

You are the Mother of fair Love.

You are the Mother of Jesus, the source of all grace,
the perfume of every virtue,
the mirror of all purity.

You are joy in weeping, victory in battle, hope in death.

How sweet your name tastes in our mouth,
how harmoniously it rings in our ears,
what rapture it brings to our hearts!

You are the happiness of the suffering,
the crown of martyrs,
the beauty of virgins.

We beg you, guide us after this exile
to possession of your Son, Jesus.

Amen.

(Visit to the Marian Shrine of the Divine Love, May 1, 1979)

Come, Spirit of Love and Peace!

Holy Spirit, most welcome guest of our hearts . . .

Spirit of truth, you who search the depths of God,
memory and prophecy in the Church,
lead mankind to recognize in Jesus of Nazareth
the Lord of glory, the Savior of the world,
the supreme fulfillment of history.

Come, Spirit of love and peace!

Creator Spirit, hidden builder of the Kingdom,
by the power of your holy gifts guide the Church . . .
to carry to the coming generations
the light of the Word who brings salvation.

Spirit of holiness, divine breath which moves the universe,
come and renew the face of the earth.
Awaken in Christians a desire for full unity,
that they may be for the world an effective sign and instrument
of intimate union with God and of the unity of the whole
human race.

Come, Spirit of love and peace!

Spirit of communion, soul and strength of the Church,
grant that wealth of charisms and ministries
may contribute to the unity of the Body of Christ;
grant that laity, consecrated persons and ordained ministers
may work together in harmony to build the one Kingdom of God.

Spirit of consolation, unfailing source of joy and peace,
inspire solidarity with the poor,
grant the sick the strength they need,
pour our trust and hope upon those experiencing trials,
awaken in all hearts a commitment to a better future.

Come, Spirit of love and peace!

Spirit of wisdom, inspiration of minds and hearts,
direct science and technology
to the service of life, justice and peace.
Render fruitful our dialogue with the followers of other religions,
lead the different cultures to appreciate the values of the Gospel.

Spirit of life, by whose power the Word was made flesh
in the womb of the Virgin Mary, the woman of attentive silence,
make us docile to the promptings of your love
and ever ready to accept the signs of the times
which you place along the paths of history.

Come, Spirit of love and peace!

To you, Spirit of love,
with the Almighty Father and the Only-Begotten Son,
be praise, honor and glory
for ever and ever. Amen.

(Prayer for the Second Year of Preparation for the Great Jubilee of
the Year 2000)

PRAYERS BY POPE FRANCIS

A Prayer for Our Earth

All-powerful God, you are present in the whole universe
and in the smallest of your creatures.

You embrace with your tenderness all that exists.

Pour out upon us the power of your love,
that we may protect life and beauty.

Fill us with peace, that we may live
as brothers and sisters, harming no one.

O God of the poor,
help us to rescue the abandoned and forgotten of this earth,
so precious in your eyes.

Bring healing to our lives,
that we may protect the world and not prey on it,
that we may sow beauty, not pollution and destruction.

Touch the hearts
of those who look only for gain
at the expense of the poor and the earth.

Teach us to discover the worth of each thing,
to be filled with awe and contemplation,
to recognize that we are profoundly united
with every creature
as we journey towards your infinite light.

We thank you for being with us each day.

Encourage us, we pray, in our struggle
for justice, love and peace.

(*Laudato Si'*, no. 246)

A Christian Prayer in Union with Creation

Father, we praise you with all your creatures.
They came forth from your all-powerful hand;
they are yours, filled with your presence and your tender love.
Praise be to you!

Son of God, Jesus,
through you all things were made.
You were formed in the womb of Mary our Mother,
you became part of this earth,
and you gazed upon this world with human eyes.
Today you are alive in every creature
in your risen glory.
Praise be to you!

Holy Spirit, by your light
you guide this world towards the Father's love
and accompany creation as it groans in travail.
You also dwell in our hearts
and you inspire us to do what is good.
Praise be to you!

Triune Lord, wondrous community of infinite love,
teach us to contemplate you
in the beauty of the universe,
for all things speak of you.
Awaken our praise and thankfulness
for every being that you have made.
Give us the grace to feel profoundly joined
to everything that is.

God of love, show us our place in this world
as channels of your love
for all the creatures of this earth,
for not one of them is forgotten in your sight.

Enlighten those who possess power and money
that they may avoid the sin of indifference,
that they may love the common good, advance the weak,
and care for this world in which we live.
The poor and the earth are crying out.

O Lord, seize us with your power and light,
help us to protect all life,
to prepare for a better future,
for the coming of your Kingdom
of justice, peace, love and beauty.
Praise be to you!
Amen.

(*Laudato Si'*, no. 246)

Prayer for Peace

Lord God of peace, hear our prayer!

We have tried so many times and over so many years to resolve our conflicts by our own powers and by the force of our arms. How many moments of hostility and darkness have we experienced; how much blood has been shed; how many lives have been shattered; how many hopes have been buried… But our efforts have been in vain.

Now, Lord, come to our aid! Grant us peace, teach us peace; guide our steps in the way of peace. Open our eyes and our hearts, and give us the courage to say: "Never again war!"; "With war everything is lost." Instill in our hearts the courage to take concrete steps to achieve peace.

Lord, God of Abraham, God of the Prophets, God of Love, you created us and you call us to live as brothers and sisters. Give us the strength daily to be instruments of peace; enable us to see everyone who crosses our path as our brother or sister. Make us sensitive to the plea of our citizens who entreat us to turn our weapons of war into implements of peace, our trepidation into confident trust, and our quarreling into forgiveness.

Keep alive within us the flame of hope, so that with patience and perseverance we may opt for dialogue and reconciliation. In this way may peace triumph at last, and may the words "division," "hatred" and "war" be banished from the heart of every man and woman. Lord, defuse the violence of our tongues and our hands. Renew our hearts and minds, so that the word which always brings us together will be "brother," and our way of life will always be that of: Shalom, Peace, Salaam!

Amen.

(Invocation for Peace, June 8, 2014)

Prayer to the Immaculate

Virgin most holy and immaculate,
to you, the honor of our people,
and the loving protector of our city,
do we turn with loving trust.

You are all-beautiful, O Mary!
In you there is no sin.

Awaken in all of us a renewed desire for holiness:
May the splendor of truth shine forth in our words,
the song of charity resound in our works,
purity and chastity abide in our hearts and bodies,
and the full beauty of the Gospel be evident in our lives.

You are all-beautiful, O Mary!
In you the Word of God became flesh.

Help us always to heed the Lord's voice:
May we never be indifferent to the cry of the poor,
or untouched by the sufferings of the sick and those in need;
may we be sensitive to the loneliness of the elderly and the vulner-
ability of children,
and always love and cherish the life of every human being.

You are all-beautiful, O Mary!
In you is the fullness of joy born of life with God.

Help us never to forget the meaning of our earthly journey:
May the kindly light of faith illumine our days,
the comforting power of hope direct our steps,
the contagious warmth of love stir our hearts;
and may our gaze be fixed on God, in whom true joy is found.

You are all-beautiful, O Mary!
Hear our prayer, graciously hear our plea:
May the beauty of God's merciful love in Jesus abide in our hearts,
and may this divine beauty save us, our city and the entire world.

Amen.

(Act of Veneration to the Blessed Virgin Mary at the Spanish
Steps, Solemnity of the Immaculate Conception, Dec. 8, 2013)

Prayer to Mary for the Amazon Region

Mother of life,
in your maternal womb Jesus took flesh,
the Lord of all that exists.
Risen, he transfigured you by his light
and made you the Queen of all creation.
For that reason, we ask you, Mary, to reign
in the beating heart of Amazonia.

Show yourself the Mother of all creatures,
in the beauty of the flowers, the rivers,
the great river that courses through it
and all the life pulsing in its forests.
Tenderly care for this explosion of beauty.

Ask Jesus to pour out all his love
on the men and women who dwell there,
that they may know how to appreciate and care for it.

Bring your Son to birth in their hearts,
so that he can shine forth in the Amazon region,
in its peoples and in its cultures,
by the light of his word,
by his consoling love,
by his message of fraternity and justice.

And at every Eucharist,
may all this awe and wonder be lifted up
to the glory of the Father.

Mother, look upon the poor of the Amazon region,
for their home is being destroyed by petty interests.
How much pain and misery,
how much neglect and abuse there is
in this blessed land
overflowing with life!

Touch the hearts of the powerful,
for, even though we sense that the hour is late,
you call us to save
what is still alive.

Mother whose heart is pierced,
who yourself suffer in your mistreated sons and daughters,
and in the wounds inflicted on nature,

reign in the Amazon,
together with your Son.

Reign so that no one else can claim lordship
over the handiwork of God.

We trust in you, Mother of life.
Do not abandon us
in this dark hour.

Amen.

(Post-Synodal Apostolic Exhortation *Querida Amazonia*, no. 111)